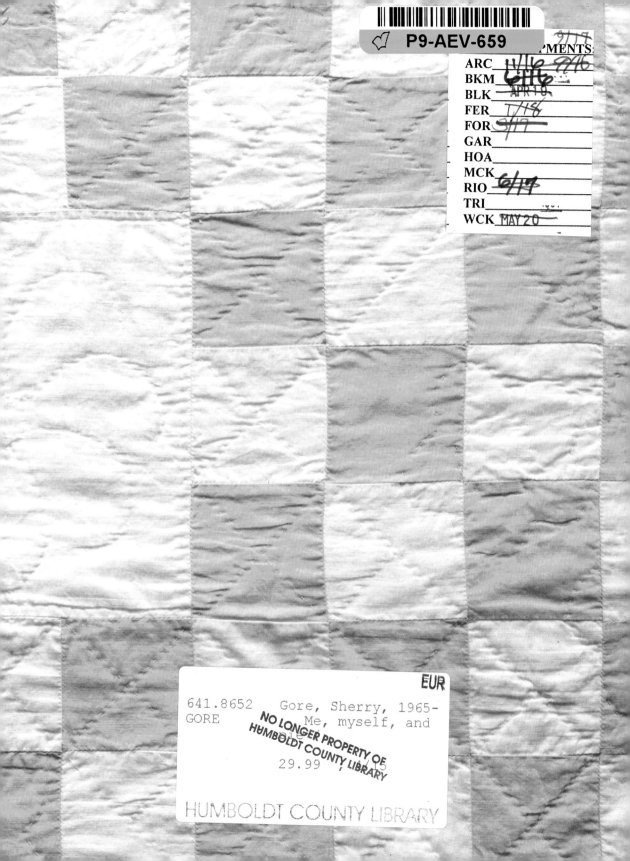

Me,
Myself,
and Pie

Me, Myself, and Pie

Sherry Gore

ZONDERVAN®

ZONDERVAN

Me, Myself, and Pie
Copyright © 2014 by Sherry Gore

Requests for information should be addressed to:
Zondervan, *Grand Rapids, Michigan 49530*

Library of Congress Cataloging-in-Publication Data

A catalog record for this book is available from the Library of Congress.

Author is represented by The Steve Laube Agency, LLC, 5025 N. Central Ave. # 635, Phoenix, Arizona 85012

Cover design: Kathy Mitchell Designs
Cover photography: Katie Jacobs
Interior photography: Katie Jacobs
Photographs pages 193, 197, and 238-239: Shutterstock.com
Photographs on pages 114, 116, 117, 119, and 241: Chris Meyer / Memories by Chris
Interior design: Lori Lynch
Senior Editor: Rebecca Warren

Printed in China

14 15 16 17 18 19 20 / DSC / 20 19 18 17 16 15 14 13 12 11 10 9 8 7 6 5 4 3 2

This book is dedicated to
Mary Mullett, who once said to me,
"I don't like pie," and I replied, "You
just haven't met the right one yet."

Contents

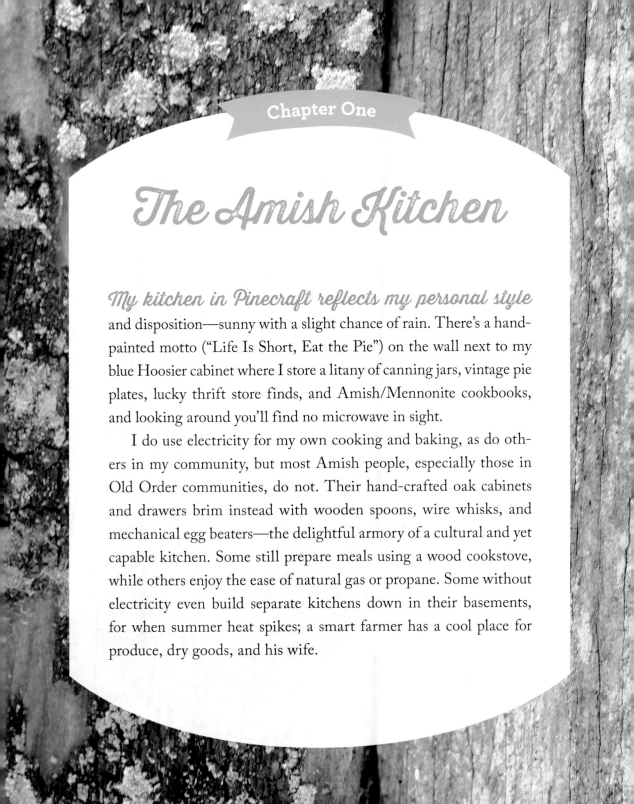

Chapter One

The Amish Kitchen

My kitchen in Pinecraft reflects my personal style and disposition—sunny with a slight chance of rain. There's a hand-painted motto ("Life Is Short, Eat the Pie") on the wall next to my blue Hoosier cabinet where I store a litany of canning jars, vintage pie plates, lucky thrift store finds, and Amish/Mennonite cookbooks, and looking around you'll find no microwave in sight.

I do use electricity for my own cooking and baking, as do others in my community, but most Amish people, especially those in Old Order communities, do not. Their hand-crafted oak cabinets and drawers brim instead with wooden spoons, wire whisks, and mechanical egg beaters—the delightful armory of a cultural and yet capable kitchen. Some still prepare meals using a wood cookstove, while others enjoy the ease of natural gas or propane. Some without electricity even build separate kitchens down in their basements, for when summer heat spikes; a smart farmer has a cool place for produce, dry goods, and his wife.

Baker's Tools

There are some items that seem destined for any Amish kitchen, no matter the locale. One is a cloth linen calendar, often embroidered with an idyllic farm scene, and just as often recycled when the year is up into a lint-free tea towel. Another is a sturdy oak dinner table, handcrafted by local craftsmen and fit for as many as thirteen or more hungry children. Then there are the dessert plates, an Amish necessity, and high chairs. And rolling pins.

    I say a girl can never have too many rolling pins. Of course I'm biased: the rolling pin is the most essential of the pie-making tools. Next would be a glass pie plate and a smooth countertop. After those, well, it gets a bit trickier, but here's a list of some basics to

help you out. It's a lot, but don't get intimidated; there's no need for the pie baking novice to invest in anything but a rolling pin and a sweet tooth.

Pastry brush	Forks	Rubber spatula	Parchment paper
Pie plates	Spoons	Beans or pie weights	Baker's twine
Mixing bowl	Baking sheet		Tin foil
Rolling pin	Pot holders		Grater
Measuring cups	Cutting board		Zester
Measuring spoons	Colander		Timer
Sharp paring knife	Egg beater		Oven thermometer
Butter knife	Mixer		
Wire whisk	Saucepan		

Basic Ingredients

Baking is a science (they don't call it "pi" for nothing), and so you want to avoid deviating too much from your recipes unless you know what you are doing (or you wish to take a walk on the wild side). Try to remember that it is the pairing of butter or shortening with other specifically listed ingredients that will really define your crust— the underlying structure of any good pie—and that substitutions in fat ingredients can severely alter the outcome of your creation. Of course, for the tastiest pies, never substitute low-fat in place of full-fat, whole ingredients. The fat is where the flavor is, after all. It's a cliché, but it's true.

When storing pies, those of a cream variety should always be refrigerated before and after being served. Fruit pies fare better out on the countertop, but they never seem to last very long up there when baked properly. They get eaten!

Solid vegetable shortening (plain and butter-flavored)
Unsalted butter
White vinegar

Pure vanilla extract
Heavy cream
Whole milk
All-purpose flour
Granulated sugar

Light brown sugar
Powdered sugar
Cocoa powder
Eggs
Sanding sugar

Chapter Two

How to Make a Delicious Crust

This is where your pie adventure begins—with the crust. It is the crust that determines how your pie is classified in the culinary world.

There's more than one way to make a delicious crust. Some bakers utilize the most modern kitchen equipment with great results. It's a quick and efficient way to get a pie on the table. Others, like me, feel that to subject my pie crust to a food processor would be an outright assault. I need to feel my ingredients to know them. I work my crust over delicately with light, loving hands. It takes a bit longer, but in creating pies by hand, I've come to know them intimately. It's true; it's a relationship that requires time, commitment, and devotion—one that will last a lifetime.

Making Your Pie Crust

When mixing your dough ingredients, always use the least amount of water you can get away with.

Take care not to overwork the dough. Overworking the dough will leave you with a tough crust and disappointed pie eaters. Work the dough just long enough to incorporate all of the ingredients. You want to see streaks of butter or shortening in your dough. This makes for the most flavorful crust imaginable.

Place your cold dough on a lightly floured, nonstick surface. Flatten the dough a bit with floured hands. Begin rolling the dough from the center outward. Smooth the crust from the middle of the circle outward, getting rid of any bubbles and folds. Continue rolling until you have a perfectly flat circle big enough to generously cover a 9-inch pie plate. Using your rolling pin, roll up the dough and place it over the pie plate. Unroll and gently pat into place. Use a wet fingertip to patch any holes in your dough. If necessary, trim the edges with a paring knife before fluting or crimping. Pinch the crust edges together gently, rotating the pie as you work. Pressing the crust between two fingers and your thumb creates a beautiful scalloped edge, giving your pie a charming, homemade look. Don't bother trying to make your pie look store-bought or bakery perfect. You want your pie to look like you made it. Whose breath isn't taken away at the very sight of a fruit pie bubbling over the top, beckoning you to eat it? It's love in a pie pan.

For the best results, chill your pastry-filled pie plate in the refrigerator for about 10 minutes before adding your filling.

Before baking, use a sharp paring knife for scoring vents in the top pie crust. Or, for a spectacular presentation, use a cookie cutter to cut out designs in the top crust. Do this on a floured surface before laying the crust over the filled pie. Place your cut-outs on the top crust. Now is the time to add an egg or cream wash, if you are using one. Last, sprinkle with sanding sugar for sweet pies.

Blind Baking

Prebaking a pie crust is also called blind baking. This is the desired method used for frozen, custard, and cream pies.

There are two ways to prepare your crust for blind baking. Pricking the bottom of an unbaked pie crust with a fork is called docking. This prevents the bottom of the pie crust from puffing up.

You may choose to use pie weights. Pie weights are small, heavy objects used to weigh down your pie crust for prebaked pie crusts, which helps the crust bake evenly. This practice is commonly used for cream pie crusts.

Some bakers use uncooked rice or dried beans for pie weights. These make great substitutes for ceramic ball pie weights. Before filling your unbaked crust with weights, line the crust with a circle of parchment paper large enough to cover the sides of your pie pan before filling it with weights.

For a full blind bake, bake the crust at 425°F for 15 minutes. Reduce heat to 375°F. Remove the weights and return the crust to the oven until the desired color is achieved. Watch the crust carefully, because this won't take long.

Decorative Edges

You can create a surprising amount of variety with your edging techniques using very simple methods and tools. Be adventurous, combining some or all of these techniques to create pies that are uniquely yours!

Fancy Techniques

Pastry cut-outs and braids are the most time-consuming decorations, but they are also the most striking. You can braid strips of dough together and press the braid firmly onto the edge of the crust to create an elegant presentation.

Hand Techniques

Creating patterns with your fingers is simple and quick, and offers an array of stylings just by using slight variations with your hands.

Cutlery Techniques

Using forks and knives, you can quickly elevate your pie edges from boring to beautiful. Using forks and spoons offers an easy way to create geometric patterns. Have fun experimenting with your utensil drawer!

Wash Recipes

Whether you use an egg or cream wash on your pies, apply the wash to an unbaked crust just before placing in the oven. Applying the wash too soon will make your crust soggy and cause it to shrink down the sides of the plate. Using a cream wash gives your crust a golden-brown matte finish. This is my favorite method. You'll want to experiment to discover yours.

For an even appearance, brush the wash into all of the nooks and crannies of your crust. An egg wash gives your pie a dark, glossy appearance. Brush your egg wash on the crust just before baking.

1 egg yolk and 1 teaspoon water combined

1 egg yolk mixed with 3 tablespoons heavy cream

3 tablespoons
heavy cream

1 egg yolk, 1 teaspoon
milk, and pinch of
salt combined

1 egg white

Pie Plates

Pie plates provide more than just a receptacle for delicious desserts. The material the pie plate is made of directly affects the consistency of the crust.

Dark Metal

Dark metal absorbs more heat than lighter metal, producing crisper crusts. Your crust may cook more quickly, so adjust your baking time as necessary.

Metal

Metal pie plates are often cheap, lightweight, and durable. These are great for a variety of pies, but make sure the metal is strong enough to support the weight of your pie. Very acidic fillings may react with the metal, so choose your filling wisely. Metal conducts heat unevenly, so the crust may not cook uniformly.

Ceramic

Ceramic conducts heat just as well as glass, but this material allows for a beautifully decorated plate as well as a pie! If you are using a particularly thick ceramic dish, you may need to adjust your baking time accordingly.

Glass

Glass conducts heat evenly, making it easy to achieve a consistently cooked crust (and filling), and the ability to check the color of the crust while it bakes is invaluable.

Disposable Aluminum

These plates are great for picnics and potlucks, but be careful not to overload the plate with filling. You may need to place the pie plate on a baking sheet to get the crust to cook evenly.

Pastry Crust

This flaky and decorative crust is a mainstay of the pie world. Often it seems that as the crust develops so do the skills of the baker, so when you finally perfect this recipe, you will have reached a level of true artistry—a Piecasso is born.

INGREDIENTS

2 cups all-purpose flour

1 tablespoon sugar (for sweet pies only)

1 teaspoon salt

3/4 cup + 2 tablespoons butter-flavored vegetable shortening, chilled

5 tablespoons ice-cold water

1 tablespoon vinegar

TO PREPARE

Blend flour, sugar, and salt well in a large bowl. Cut the shortening into pea-sized pieces and work into flour mixture until crumbs form. In a separate bowl, mix together cold water and vinegar. Gradually add the water mixture to the flour mixture until combined. Shape the dough into a ball, cover in plastic wrap, and chill for at least 30 minutes.

On a lightly floured surface, roll out the dough to a uniform thickness. Place in a pie plate and trim the edges.

Bake at 400°F for 8–12 minutes, or until golden brown. Let cool. Makes two 9-inch pie crusts.

Sue's Single Pastry Crust

This old homemade recipe still makes thousands of appearances on Amish windowsills across America. Who is Sue? Who knows? But if you ever find out, make sure to thank her for me.

TO PREPARE:

Place flour in a large bowl and cut in shortening. Add salt and water, and alternate adding 1 tablespoon at a time. Mix until well combined. Take care not to overwork your dough, as too much handling results in a tough crust. Gently work your dough ingredients together just long enough to fully incorporate them. You should see marbled streaks of fat once you've shaped the dough into a ball. Shape the dough into a ball, cover in plastic wrap, and chill for at least 30 minutes.

On a lightly floured surface, roll out the dough to a uniform thickness. Place in a pie plate and trim the edges.

Makes three 9-inch pie crusts.

INGREDIENTS

1 ¼ cups vegetable shortening

3 cups all-purpose flour

1 teaspoon salt

6 tablespoons cold water

Butter Pastry Crust

For butter lovers everywhere and the first choice for any baker planning a pot pie or savory pie, this crust is lighter and puffier than traditional recipes. Not to be confused with "Butter Pies," as in, "I liked everything she cooked butter pies." Don't get it? Try saying it out loud.

INGREDIENTS

3 cups all-purpose flour

1 teaspoon salt

1 cup butter, chilled and diced

6–8 tablespoons ice water

TO PREPARE

In a large bowl, combine flour and salt. Cut in butter until crumbs appear. Add water 1 tablespoon at a time. Shape the dough into a smooth ball, being careful to not overwork the dough. For best results, wrap the dough in plastic and refrigerate for at least 4 hours, or overnight.

Recipe may be halved for a single crust pie.

For a prebaked crust, bake at 400°F for 8–12 minutes, until golden brown.

Cheddar Cheese Crust

Add 1 cup of grated, sharp Cheddar cheese to the pastry crust dough ingredients before shaping into a ball.

Herbed Crust

Add 2 tablespoons of your favorite dried, crushed herbs to pastry crust dough.

Shortbread Crust

A sophisticated and debonair taste, shortbread traces back to Scotland, the land that brought us Sean Connery, and this crust pairs as nicely with fillings as he did with his leading ladies. Peach, pumpkin, strawberries, caramel, chocolate, banana cream—anything goes.

TO PREPARE

Using a large bowl, cream butter and confectioners' sugar until light and fluffy. In a separate bowl, stir together flour and baking powder; blend into butter mixture. Pat dough into a 9-inch pie pan. Bake at 350°F for 12 to 15 minutes, or until edges are lightly browned.

INGREDIENTS

1/2 cup butter, softened

1/4 cup confectioners' sugar

1 cup all-purpose flour

1/8 teaspoon baking powder

Chocolate Shortbread Crust

Supposedly a picture is worth a thousand words, unless that word is chocolate. *Then I think it's about equal.*

INGREDIENTS

1/3 cup packed firmly packed brown sugar

6 tablespoons cold butter, cut into small pieces

3/4 cup all-purpose flour

1/4 cup cocoa powder

1/2 teaspoon salt

TO PREPARE

In a large bowl, cream the sugar and butter. Add the flour, cocoa powder, and salt and mix until thoroughly combined. Pat dough into the bottom and sides of a 9-inch pie pan. Freeze the unbaked crust for 10 minutes. Bake at 350°F for 10 minutes. Remove from oven and let cool for 30 minutes before filling.

Chocolate Cookie Crust

This crust derives its palate power from a universally beloved cookie concoction, the chocolate sandwich cookie.

TO PREPARE

In a large bowl, combine all of the ingredients together. Pat onto bottom and sides of a 9-inch pie pan. Bake at 350°F for 7 to 10 minutes or until set. Remove from oven and let cool for 30 minutes.

INGREDIENTS

20 chocolate sandwich cookies, finely crushed

1/4 teaspoon salt

4 tablespoons butter

2 tablespoons milk

Graham Cracker Crust

Count on this cookie-cracker crust couplet and your guests can't help but ask for s'more.

INGREDIENTS

- 1 1/2 cups graham crackers, finely ground
- 2 tablespoons sugar
- 6 tablespoons butter, melted
- 1/8 teaspoon ground cinnamon

TO PREPARE

In a large bowl, mix all of the ingredients together. Pat into bottom and sides of a 9-inch pie pan. Bake at 375°F until golden brown for 6–7 minutes, not one minute more. Remove from the oven and let cool for 30 minutes before filling.

Pretzel Graham Cracker Crust

This salty-sweet crust fits wonderfully with all kinds of pies, but it is at its most mischievous when paired with either a chocolate- or strawberry-based filling.

TO PREPARE

In a large bowl, mix all of the ingredients together. Press into bottom of a pie plate. Bake at 375°F for 6–7 minutes, or until set.

INGREDIENTS

1 cup graham cracker crumbs

1 cup pretzel crumbs

1/2 cup sugar

12 tablespoons butter, melted

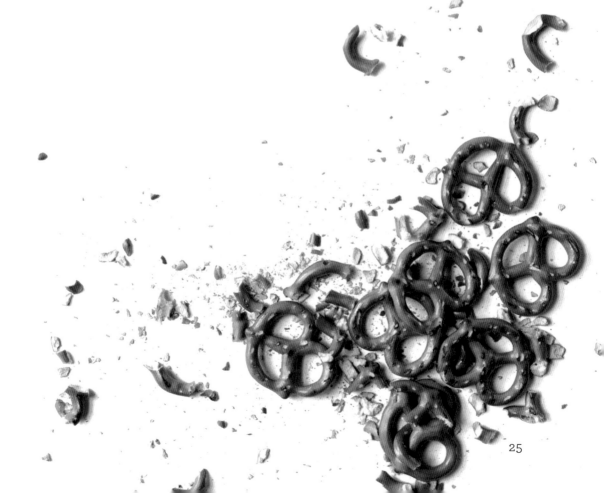

Gingersnap Crust

Gingersnaps are called "ginger nuts" in England, "pepper cookies" in Norway, and "brown biscuits" in Denmark. Everywhere else they're just called "delicious." So why not put them in a pie?

INGREDIENTS

1 1/2 heaping cups crisp (not soft) gingersnap cookie crumbs

2 tablespoons sugar

1/4 teaspoon salt

1/4 cup melted butter

TO PREPARE

In a large bowl, mix all of the ingredients together. Pat into bottom and sides of a 9-inch pie pan. Place pan in the freezer for 15 minutes, then bake at 350°F for 5 minutes. Remove from oven and let cool for 20-30 minutes before filling.

NOTE: This crust can also be made gluten-free if you use a gluten-free brand of gingersnaps.

Gluten-Free Crust

More and more foods are becoming available for our gluten-intolerant friends every day, and it would be a real shame if pie were left on the outside. After all, someone once said, "A life without pie is a life not lived." (I think it was me.)

Take 1 1/2 cups of flour mixture and add the following:

1/2 cup cold butter, cut in pieces

1 1/2 teaspoons sugar

1 teaspoon salt

5 or 6 tablespoon ice water

In a large bowl, blend all ingredients together, either by hand or in a food processor. The blended mixture should be moist and pliable. If you pinch it, the mixture should hold together. If it doesn't, add another tablespoon or two of ice water.

　　Press the completed mixture into a ball, wrap in plastic wrap, and allow it to rest in the refrigerator for about half an hour.

　　Roll out dough onto a lightly floured surface. Do not fold and re-roll to create layers because this will make your crust hard. Place crust in an ungreased pie plate and repair any tears or gaps. Minimize stretching since this crust will already shrink a fair amount. Bake at 350°F for 15 minutes for a soft crust, or 20 minutes for a crunchy one. Judge the crust by time, not by look, because it won't brown like a regular flour crust. Cool and fill. (Alternately, you can use this as a baked 2-crust pie crust, fill it, place a second crust on top, and brush the top crust with an egg wash to give it a nice color.)

1 cup sweet rice flour

1 cup potato starch (not potato flour)

1 cup cornstarch

1/2 cup cornflour (You can use masa for this; the lime doesn't hurt the recipe)

1/2 cup tapioca flour (or tapioca starch)

4 teaspoons xanthan gum

A Slice of Amish Life: My Pie Story

The first time I tasted pie, I knew it wasn't for me. Not Sherry Gore. I was young and the pie store-bought. Cherry. And I like cherries. But I didn't trust this pie. It came from a freezer in a flimsy metal pan, with a perfect circle cut in the top. When the pie came out of the oven, the bottom was black, like the crust had gone through a chemical reaction. It was pie when it went in . . . What was it now?

I tried to slice a piece but it wouldn't budge. I wrenched back and forth with all my strength until a small lump broke free. But the filling still clung to the pan; it wouldn't give up the crust. I pulled harder. It wouldn't give. I pulled again, and it broke with a *snap*. Bizarrely, most of the filling had snapped back into the pie. Actually snapped back.

What planet is this from? I wondered.

Finally I tasted it. *Ugh*. Rubber cement. *Cherry* rubber cement. I chewed and chewed, but the elastic pie still filled my mouth. It wasn't getting smaller. In fact, there was somehow *more* of it. My jaw started to ache. I kept chewing. The pain spread across my face. I felt like I'd run a marathon with my cheeks. Still I chewed.

I might be stuck with this piece of cherry pie forever, I thought. *I'll have to learn sign language.*

Eventually, I surrendered and spit that synthetic mess into the trash. I didn't swallow any. It might be why I'm still alive today.

After that, I avoided pie. For years. I'd stand around dessert trays like a teenage girl who still thinks boys are dumb, watching my friends go crazy and wondering, *Why all the fuss?*

Years later, when I moved our family to Pinecraft, we attended Sunnyside Fellowship, a "plain" Beachy Amish-Mennonite church. At Sunnyside, service lasts for two hours, and then afterward the congregation shares a meal together. It's a wonderful tradition, enabling us to glorify God and eat heartily—my two favorite things.

We call the meal a "carry-in," because the women "carry in" food as the men set tables and chairs. There's always a lot of fried chicken, and there's always homemade pie.

Amish and Mennonite women take great pride in their pies; many have a top-secret, devastating recipe saved for desperate situations. A sugar bomb. For use only when all other options have been exhausted. Carry-ins are the testing sites for those nuclear recipes.

Of course, this didn't matter to me; I'd forsaken pie. I was a brownie girl. I was cool with cake.

But during my first carry-in, I noticed those pies were different: big, fluffy, creamy, and brighter than the sun. One had sugar droplets like rhinestones. None resembled rubber cement.

It came into my head to try one. This is called "divine inspiration." I was having a road-to-Damascus moment.

There was a little peach number that caught my eye. Nothing special. It's not my favorite fruit. It didn't have the color of the grape or the smell of the apple. It was a humble pie. And I was about to have mine.

I fetched a small paper plate and a slice of the peach. It was gorgeous: a golden brown crust gathering peach slivers and syrup in a tight embrace, smoothing them into a thick molasses, and scented in cinnamon and sugarcane.

I dipped a spoon into the pie and closed my lips around it. Hot, tangy steam billowed against the roof of my mouth and escaped through my nose. I withdrew the spoon carefully, unsure whether my tongue could bear such intensity. For a moment, I puffed my cheeks and let the pie sit, sugar tickling against my gums.

Then I bit into it.

Wow.

What do you think it feels like to look back-ward from the shuttle, and view Earth from space? You'd probably say something like: "I just never knew . . ." Well, this taste was like that. Cosmic. My face paled, and my toes jerked. A fresh fruit pleasure drank me up from the inside out. I was full-bodied peach. Peach steam whistled from my pores like in a cartoon, and I slumped against the chair.

I sure was glad I'd gone to church that morning, because I might've just died and gone to heaven.

I couldn't move for five minutes flat, and the next time I did, it was to look at the rest of those pies. Custard orbited a fresh strawberry. A key lime burned as yellow as a comet. Gravity from the sour cherry drew us all in.

Each pie was its own new universe.

Calm yourself, I thought. *No use having a pie panic attack. Remember to breathe.* I couldn't just load up on all those pies. It wasn't polite. I would have to wait.

But only until next Sunday.

In 2001, our family moved to Burkesville, Kentucky, to live in a wonderful Amish community just north of the Cumberland River. Jacinda (the oldest), Shannon (the middle child), and Tyler (the baby) lived with me in a small trailer set deep off the road. It was in a cow pasture. It was our little oasis.

We didn't have much and made due with what we had. As usual, I looked to food for financial salvation. I was so excited to be reintroduced to pie that I made it my goal to sell them at the local flea market.

I didn't know how to make any, so my friend Rosanna Esh taught me to bake fried pies, a delicious fried treat made with dried apples, or what we call "apple snitz." She showed me how to soak the apples in a little water and spice (cinnamon, allspice, and nutmeg for starters), and then add sugar, flour, and butter. The syrup around the apples soaks up flavor and thickens into a nice, gooey filling. The apples are then chopped, mixed with the filling, and fried in a fold-over pie crust.

I'd never eaten a fried pie before, but I knew Rosanna's recipes were winners. She'd offered me gold, and I was going to take it.

Jacinda has always been a farmgirl, and in Kentucky she spent her time out in the fields, working the cows, sheep, horses, and land around us, often with tiny Tyler alongside, nipping at her knees. So it was Shannon who helped me in the kitchen and with the housework. She was a born homemaker.

On Fridays, Shannon and I made as many pies as we could—usually around one hundred. It was very labor intensive. We first made the dough from scratch, and then we'd roll it flat and cut out individual circles. We never wasted any trimmings or any scraps—everything went right back into that dough.

Each hand-rolled crust became a peach, apple, or cherry pie. Shannon made the fillings while I stood at the stove. We didn't have a deep fryer, and our cast-iron skillet was only big enough to hold two fried pies at a time, so it took us at least fifty batches to make one hundred pies. Each batch took six minutes to cook. It made for a long day.

We'd glaze half of the pies and then carefully wrap each one in plastic. The finished pies couldn't be stacked, so by late afternoon on Friday our entire kitchen, from table to countertop, cabinets to chairs, overflowed with individually wrapped fried pies.

Every cabinet had dried dough on the handle. Every wall was covered in flour.

On Saturdays, I'd hire a driver to haul me, myself, and my pie seventy miles to the flea market. We'd get $1.25 for each one.

It was our weekly income. For almost a year. Pie and I had started a life together. And it worked.

In Pinecraft, it's a tradition to line up outside Yoder's Restaurant on Thanksgiving Day. By 6:00 a.m., hundreds of people fill the sidewalk. It's a madhouse. There are security guards and news cameras. What is everyone after? Fresh homemade pie, of course.

Everyone wants to serve a savory Dutch apple crumb, or Southern pecan, or butterscotch cream after dinner, and Yoder's has the best pies around. People drive in from Tampa to get their hands on those pies, some ordering twenty at a time.

The lines are so long that Yoder's hires cute little Amish girls to hand out samples, and when she was young, my daughter Shannon did just that. As she got older, she worked there as a hostess.

One year she came home

with interesting news: Yoder's was hiring part-time bakers to help meet the Thanksgiving crush.

I thought it might be fun, and I had a history of making pie. It would be easy money. So I applied and I was hired on the spot, a three-day job. We'd start on Monday and finish Wednesday night, the night before Thanksgiving.

On the first morning, I got up at 4:00 a.m. in order to make it to work by 5:00. It was still dark when I arrived at Yoder's on my bicycle. The managers stationed us along thin tables behind the restaurant in the parking lot, in the freezing cold. That morning Pinecraft was as cold as I'd ever felt it, below 40 degrees for sure. We're not used to that. We might as well have been buried in snow.

Fortunately, I made a quick friend, a sharp young man by the name of Daniel Fisher. He was an intellectual: a thinker, a writer, and an Old Order bachelor with much to say. He was also very nice.

We talked at length over five-gallon buckets of frozen apple slices. Our job was to fill each pie crust with a handful of frozen apples, add flour, mix in a premade filling, and then pass the shell down to the next worker.

Before ten minutes were up my hands were on fire. Those craggy frozen apples hurt. Luckily, Daniel found us some blue latex gloves that helped immensely. But even then, I couldn't feel my hands after a few minutes of work.

By Wednesday night, we part-timers were exhausted, but we still had hundreds of pies to make. We had to buck up. None of us wanted to disappoint all those sweet-toothed sweethearts waking early to stand in line. I thought about making a speech, but "plain" workers don't need General Patton to work hard. It's in our blood. Soon we hit our second wind, and we raced forward as the hours chipped away. We were a pie chain gang, a taste locomotive that couldn't be stopped.

We made every pie they asked for, and then some. The seven of us made 1,700 pie crusts that day. By Wednesday, more than 5,100 pies were made and sold. It was intense. Pie making is not for the faint of heart.

Thanksgiving Day went off without a hitch. There were enough pies for everyone, and Yoder's was pleased with our work. Brian, one of the restaurant managers, gave me a sour cherry pie (along with a paycheck). I was just thrilled to have helped.

Once again, I'd leaned on pie for a new experience. But this time pie indirectly allowed me to experience something else, something transformative.

Pie introduced me to Daniel Fisher, my frozen apple buddy. Some years later, Daniel had the insight to create the *Pinecraft Pauper*, our community's first and only local newspaper. When he did, he called on me to write for his publication. I loved it from the start. And some time later, as he was leaving the paper to embark on another opportunity, he called on me again. This time he asked me run the newspaper as editor and publisher. I said yes.

The *Pinecraft Pauper* introduced me to publishing and inspired me to tell stories about our little Amish world in Pinecraft. It led to *Cooking & Such* magazine and my first published book, *Simply Delicious Amish Cooking*; it even led to the book you're reading right this second.

My writing career got started over pie. Because of pie. What I first hated ended up changing my life.

Chapter Three

Cream Pies

Husbands and boyfriends love cream pies, and that's a fact. The rest of America may go ga-ga over apple or cherry, but when it's time for Laurel to hit Hardy with a pie, there's only one kind that fits the bill, and it isn't shoo-fly. Cream pies dominate pie contests and have always been my favorite. Until recently I held coconut cream as the pinnacle, but after embarking on a quest for the perfect pie, I found it was a banana cream instead (and I ate the evidence).

So go be a sleuth yourself and find your favorite pie; with these recipes, and a hardy sense of adventure, you might solve a riddle that's vexed your taste buds for years. Just don't go and throw it in anybody's face (unless they ask first).

Orange Pie

This is the pie I want in heaven, a delightful concoction as bright in color as it is in taste. The surging burst of citrus combines with a tender, flaky crust and smooth filling—a true epiphany!

TO PREPARE ORANGE FILLING

Bring 1 1/2 cups of water to a boil in a saucepan. In a bowl, mix together sugar, cornstarch, and drink mix. Add 1/2 cup of water into the sugar mixture and stir. Pour into boiling water, reduce to medium heat, stirring as it cooks. Remove from heat when it begins to thicken a bit. Cool. Stir in orange pieces.

TO PREPARE CREAM CHEESE MIXTURE

In a bowl, stir together cream cheese and confectioners' sugar until creamy. Add half of the whipped cream to the mixture. Spoon into baked pie crust. Top with orange filling. Refrigerate overnight.

FOR THE GARNISH

Decorate the top of the pie with the reserved whipped cream, if desired.

FOR THE CRUST

One 9-inch baked pastry pie crust

INGREDIENTS

2 cups water

1 cup sugar

2 tablespoons cornstarch

1 teaspoon orange-flavored drink mix

3 oranges, peeled and chopped

CREAM CHEESE MIXTURE

4 ounces cream cheese, softened

2 cups confectioners' sugar

8 ounces whipped cream

8 ounces whipped cream (optional)

Strawberry Cream Pie

A summertime combination of classic flavors, this "strawberry blonde" is simple enough for the amateur baker but fit for the most special of occasions. For a zesty twist on an all-time classic recipe, try a pretzel or cookie crust. Your guests won't complain.

FOR THE CRUST

2 tablespoons milk

1/2 cup vegetable oil

1 1/2 cups flour

1 1/2 tablespoons sugar

1 teaspoon salt

INGREDIENTS

2 cups water

1 cup sugar

2 rounded tablespoons arrowroot flour (or cornstarch)

1 (3-ounce) box strawberry gelatin

Garnish

1 pound fresh strawberries, stemmed, hulled, and sliced, plus extra for garnish

whipped cream (optional)

TO PREPARE CRUST

In a pie pan, mix milk and oil. Blend in flour, sugar, and salt, then press in bottom and sides of pan. Bake at 350°F for 15–25 minutes, or until light brown.

TO PREPARE FILLING

Boil water, sugar, and arrowroot flour in a saucepan over high heat. Add gelatin, reduce heat to medium, and stir until the mixture thickens. Let cool until warm but not hot.

Add the strawberries to the glaze when it is warm but not set.

Pour the strawberry mixture into the baked pie crust. Chill for at least 2 hours, or until fully set and chilled.

FOR THE GARNISH

Decorate pie with whipped cream and extra strawberries, if desired.

TIP: Use a pretzel crust (p. 25) for a fun twist on this pie. The sweet and salt combination is wonderful!

Coconut Cream Pie

This is called the "boyfriend pie" because it's the one that gets a girl noticed. My Amish friend Fannie is famous for this treat, and when made with loving hands, the coconut cream is a shoo-in winner at a pie contest. That coconut flavor! So decadent!

TO PREPARE

Preheat oven to 350°F. In a bowl, dissolve gelatin in cold water. Set aside.

In a saucepan, mix sugar, flour, and salt. Gradually stir in 1 1/2 cups milk. Add egg yolks. Cook over low heat until boiling, stirring constantly. Remove from heat; stir in the dissolved gelatin. Cool until partly set. Stir in vanilla. Fold in whipped cream and flaked coconut. Pour mixture into pie crust.

In a separate bowl, combine the egg whites and cream of tartar. Beat until stiff. Add the sugar and beat until soft peaks form. Fold in flaked coconut. Next, gently add the meringue on top of the custard mixture. Bake at for 350°F for 12–15 minutes, until meringue and coconut are a golden color.

Let cool for 1 hour on a wire rack. Refrigerate for at least 3 hours before serving.

TIP: For a deep-dish pie plate or for added height and deliciousness, double the meringue recipe.

FOR THE CRUST

One 9-inch baked pastry pie crust

INGREDIENTS

1 package unflavored gelatin

1/4 cup water

1/2 cup sugar

1/4 cup all-purpose flour

1/2 teaspoon salt

1 1/2 cups milk

3 large egg yolks

1 teaspoon vanilla extract

1 cup whipped topping or whipped cream

1 cup toasted flaked coconut

MERINGUE

3 large egg whites

1/4 teaspoon cream of tartar

1/2 cup sugar

1 cup flaked coconut

Banana Cream Pie

This American favorite is a beloved treat among the Amish. A classic pie, the banana cream needs no improvement (but if you're feeling frisky, try sprinkling chocolate or peanut butter chips on top for a bit of pure genius).

FOR THE CRUST

One 9-inch baked pastry pie crust

INGREDIENTS

2 1/3 cups milk, divided

1 cup sugar

1/4 cup cornstarch

dash of salt

3 large egg yolks

2 bananas, sliced in rounds

whipped cream

TO PREPARE

Bring 2 cups of milk to a boil in a saucepan over medium-high heat. Mix sugar, cornstarch, and salt together in a bowl. Add egg yolks and 1/3 cup milk and mix well. Stir cornstarch mixture into milk and bring back to a boil, stirring constantly. Remove from the heat and let cool. Place 1 sliced banana on bottom of baked pie crust. Spoon the cooled pudding on top of the bananas. Top with whipped cream.

FOR THE GARNISH

Top with 1 sliced banana just before serving.

For a heaping, full pie or a deep-dish pie, I like to double the pudding recipe

TIP: For an elegant and unexpected presentation, slice the bananas lengthwise.

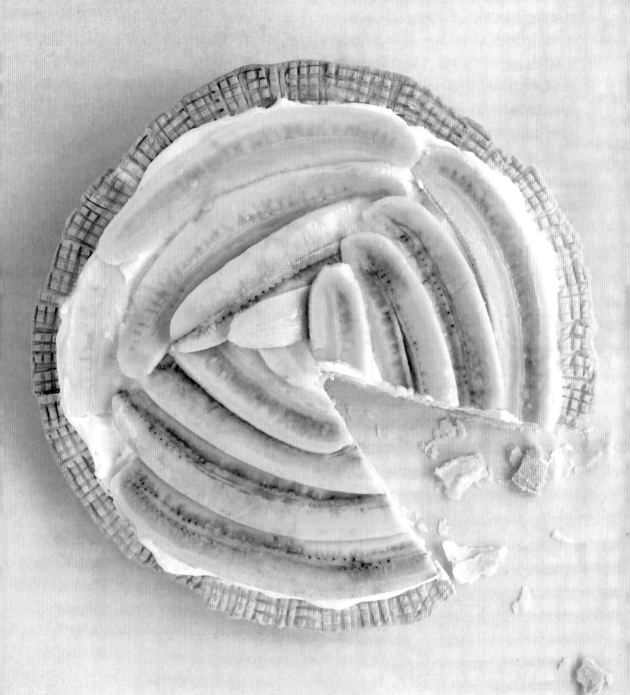

Dutch Peaches and Cream Pie

If you're a fan of peach pie, this one will take you right back in time. It's a traditional Pennsylvania Dutch recipe and, boy, were they on to something special. A crumb topping covers soft peaches; a smart host puts a scoop of vanilla ice cream on the side.

TO PREPARE

Preheat oven to 425°F. Combine brown sugar, flour, and salt in a small bowl. Sprinkle the mixture over the peaches in a separate bowl. Add the cream and gently stir. Pour mixture into the unbaked pie crust. Top with your favorite crumb recipe. Bake at 425°F for 10 minutes, then lower heat to 350°F and bake for 30 minutes. Let cool and then chill in the refrigerator until ready to serve.

FOR THE GARNISH

Top with whipped cream and vanilla ice cream.

FOR THE CRUST

One 9-inch unbaked pastry pie crust

INGREDIENTS

3/4 cup firmly packed brown sugar

1/4 cup all-purpose flour

1/4 teaspoon salt

4 cups fresh peaches, peeled and sliced

3/4 cup heavy cream

Crumb topping (p. 257–261)

Lemon Blueberry Cream Pie

Lemons and blueberries must be friends because they sure do bring out the best in each other. For those who like some zip in their sweets, or some sweet in their zip, it is the contrast that makes this pie a triumph. Case closed: Opposites DO attract.

FOR THE CRUST

One 9-inch baked pastry or shortbread crust

INGREDIENTS

1 cup sugar

3 tablespoons cornstarch

1 cup milk

3 large eggs yolks, beaten

1/4 cup butter

1 tablespoon grated lemon zest, plus extra for garnish

1/4 cup lemon juice

8 ounces sour cream

2 cups fresh blueberries, washed and stemmed, plus extra for garnish

TO PREPARE

In a saucepan, combine sugar and cornstarch. Add milk, egg yolks, butter, and lemon zest and cook over medium heat. Cook and stir until thick and bubbly; continue cooking for 2 minutes, stirring constantly. Remove from the heat. Stir in the lemon juice. Refrigerate mixture until completely cool. Pour the chilled mixture into the pie crust. In a bowl, gently fold the sour cream and blueberries together. Combine with the cooled cream and pour the entire mixture into the pie crust. Chill at least 4 hours. When serving, top with blueberries and lemon zest, if you like.

TOPPING VARIATION

Add sweetened whipped cream and fresh lemon slices.

Peanut Butter Cream Pie

Introducing the champion: the number one most-asked-for pie in Pinecraft Amish restaurants. Close the windows and lock up the doors when baking, because this royal patriarch has a wonderful peanut aroma that they just don't sell in stores. Remember to use a large dessert plate when serving, and you might want to keep a glass of cold milk close by as well. It's good to be king.

TO PREPARE

Bring 2 cups of milk to a boil in a saucepan over medium-high heat. In a bowl, mix sugar, cornstarch, and salt together. Stir in 1/2 cup milk, add egg yolks, and mix well. Stir cornstarch mixture into the boiling milk. Bring back to a boil, stirring constantly. Remove from heat and cool.

TO MAKE CRUMBS

In a bowl, mix together confectioners' sugar and peanut butter until crumbly. Reserve 1/3 of the crumbs for the top of the pie. Put remaining crumbs in the bottom of the baked pie crust. Pour the cooled filling on top of the crumbs. Cover with whipped topping. Sprinkle the remaining crumbs on top.

FOR THE CRUST

One 9-inch baked pastry pie crust

INGREDIENTS

2 1/2 cups milk, divided

1 cup sugar

1/4 cup cornstarch

dash of salt

3 large egg yolks

FOR THE CRUMBS

1 1/2 cups confectioners' sugar

1/2 cup peanut butter

whipped topping

Vanilla Cream Pie

Simplicity, simplicity, simplicity. When custard and vanilla are in cahoots, there's just no need for anything else.

FOR THE CRUST

One 9-inch baked
pastry pie crust

INGREDIENTS

2 1/2 cups milk, divided

1 cup sugar

1/4 cup cornstarch

dash of salt

3 large egg yolks,
beaten

whipped cream

TO PREPARE

Bring 2 cups milk to a boil in a saucepan over medium-high heat. Mix sugar, cornstarch, and salt together in a bowl. Stir in a 1/2 cup of milk. Add the egg yolks and mix well. Stir the cornstarch mixture into the boiling milk and bring back to a boil, stirring constantly. The pudding is ready when it coats the back of a spoon. Remove from the heat and let cool in bowl. Once the pudding is cooled, pour into the baked pie crust and refrigerate overnight, or until set.

FOR THE GARNISH

Top with thick layer of whipped cream.

VARIATION

For an extra burst of flavor, add the seeds from half of a vanilla bean to the pudding. It not only tastes amazing, it also smells wonderful.

Chocolate Cream Pudding Pie

The first bite is the one that surprises. Chocolate floats in on pudding as cool as a crystal lake, followed by a crunchy crust. Sure to please chocolate lovers young and old, though we all know chocolate lovers are ageless.

TO PREPARE

Bring 2 cups milk to a boil in a saucepan over medium-high heat. Mix sugar, cornstarch, salt, and cocoa together in a bowl. Stir in 1/2 cup milk. Mix well. Stir the cocoa mixture into the boiling milk. Bring to a boil, stirring constantly. Remove from the heat and cool. Pour into the baked pie crust and refrigerate until the pudding has set.

FOR THE GARNISH

Top with whipped cream, if desired.

TIP: To create an elegant version of this pie, double the recipe (using the chocolate cookie crust) and use a springform pan.

FOR THE CRUST

One chocolate cookie, chocolate shortbread, shortbread, or baked pastry crust

INGREDIENTS

2 1/2 cups milk, divided

1 cup sugar

1/4 cup cornstarch

dash salt

1/4 cup cocoa powder

whipped cream (optional)

Chocolate Peanut Butter Banana Cream Pie

Its name is a mouthful, but as soon as you lay eyes on this multi-adjective polyglot, you'll have a mouthful too.

FOR THE CRUST

One 9-inch baked pastry, chocolate shortbread, or chocolate cookie crust

INGREDIENTS

2 1/2 ounces semisweet chocolate squares, divided

1/2 cup creamy peanut butter

3 bananas, cut lengthwise in half, then crosswise into quarters

double recipe of homemade vanilla pudding (p. 55)

2 cups whipped cream, divided

TO PREPARE

Melt 1 1/2 ounces chocolate and the peanut butter in double boiler. Place bananas in crust; drizzle with melted chocolate. Let cool.

Prepare pudding. Let cool. Stir in 1 cup whipped cream. Spread over bananas. Refrigerate 4 hours.

FOR THE GARNISH

Top with reserved whipped cream and chocolate curls just before serving.

Candy Bar Pie

Candy Bar pie. An endless variety of candy bars can make up this delectable treat, and guess what—you get to pick!

TO PREPARE

Make the pudding and let it cool. Fold in whipped topping and candy bars. Pour into pie crust and refrigerate for at least 4 hours, or overnight.

TIP: For an impressive pie sure to please everyone, double the filling recipe.

FOR THE CRUST

One 9-inch baked pastry, chocolate cookie, or chocolate shortbread recipe

INGREDIENTS

6 ounces chocolate pudding (make your own or use store-bought)

3 cups frozen whipped topping

4 full-size candy bars, roughly chopped

Praline Cream Pie

Pralines are naturally sweet, but don't fret if you're afraid this pie will be too rich—the cream pudding brings it back down to earth. Luckily, that's where you are. Enjoy.

FOR THE CRUST

One 9-inch baked pastry pie crust

INGREDIENTS

1/3 cup butter

1/3 cup firmly packed brown sugar

1/2 cup chopped pecans

1 recipe (2 1/2 cups) homemade vanilla pudding (p. 55)

2 cups whipped topping

TO PREPARE

In a saucepan over low heat, cook butter, brown sugar, and pecans together until sugar is dissolved and mixture is bubbly. Pour into pie crust and let cool.

Spoon pudding over cooled pie crust.

FOR THE GARNISH

Top with whipped cream and candied pecans for extra crunch.

Grasshopper Pie

It's not a coincidence that this pie jumps off your fork and onto your tongue, or at least that's what it feels like when this spry mix of healthy mint and milk chocolate arrives. Chirp, chirp.

TO PREPARE

In a large bowl, whip together marshmallow crème, peppermint extract, and food coloring until smooth and a uniform mint green color. In a separate bowl, whip cream until soft peaks form, then fold into marshmallow mixture. Pour mixture into pan and freeze at least 2 hours, until firm. Remove from freezer 20 minutes before serving to soften slightly.

FOR THE GARNISH

Sprinkle pie with chocolate cookie crumbs and top with chocolate after-dinner mints.

TIP: Use small springform pans to create multiple cakes that can be topped with different garnishes.

FOR THE CRUST

One 9-inch baked chocolate cookie crust

INGREDIENTS

2 cups store-bought marshmallow crème

2 teaspoons peppermint extract

about 4 drops green food color

2 cups sweetened whipping cream

1/2 cup chocolate cookie crumbs

About 12 chocolate after-dinner mints, for garnish

Cookies and Cream Ice-Cream Pie

A gorgeous conflation of two iconic desserts, cookies and cream, enjoy most of their fame from starring roles in ice-cream tubs across the world. But they learned their delicious dance here, in a creamy pie filling. Do yourself a favor and go back to where it all began.

FOR THE CRUST

One 9-inch prepared chocolate cookie crust

INGREDIENTS

14 chocolate cream cookies, whole

1/2 gallon vanilla ice cream

3/4 cup prepared fudge sauce, divided

TO PREPARE

Line the cookies up in a circular fashion on top of the pie crust. Press firmly into the pan. Freeze for at least 1 hour. Take ice cream out of the freezer so that it can soften, about 10–15 minutes. Spread half of the ice cream over the cookies. Drizzle half of the fudge sauce over ice cream. Freeze for 1 hour. Spread the remaining ice cream over the top. Drizzle with the reserved fudge. Freeze for 4 hours or overnight. Let set for 15–20 minutes before serving.

TIP: For an elegant presentation, use a springform pan to create this pie.

Raisin Cream Pie

A staple in Amish communities, the raisin cream pie comes equipped with everything needed to satisfy a sweet tooth, and you're probably already equipped to make it. This simple recipe uses items found in the everyday workabout kitchen because it has been passed down from Amish mother to daughter for decades, and why not? The raisins anchor the smooth, creamy taste; they burst at each bite.

TO PREPARE

Plump the raisins by soaking them in about 1 cup of boiling hot water. This takes about 15 minutes. Drain and set aside.

Beat egg yolks in a bowl. Add the salt, sugar, and flour and beat until smooth.

Pour milk into a saucepan, add egg mixture and butter, and mix together.

Stirring constantly, cook mixture over medium heat for about 15 minutes until it thickens, starts to boil, and has a smooth texture. Don't leave it to cook on its own without stirring.

Sprinkle the raisins over the pie crust and pour in the hot milk and egg mixture. Chill 2 to 3 hours before serving.

FOR THE GARNISH

Serve with whipped cream, if desired.

FOR THE CRUST

One 9-inch baked pastry pie crust

INGREDIENTS

1/4 cup raisins

4 large egg yolks

1/8 teaspoon salt

1/2 cup sugar

2 tablespoons all-purpose flour

2 cups milk

1 tablespoon butter

whipped cream (optional)

Pumpkin Gingersnap Cheesecake

Warm, spicy gingersnaps bring the exotic to the familiar with this sassy alternative to traditional pumpkin pie. But don't just slip this recipe in on Thanksgiving without telling anybody, for they may take one bite and never go back.

FOR THE CRUST

One gingersnap, graham cracker, or chocolate shortbread crust

INGREDIENTS

2 (8-ounce) packages cream cheese, softened

1/4 cup firmly packed brown sugar

1/4 cup white sugar

1 teaspoon maple syrup (or 1/2 teaspoon maple flavoring)

2 large eggs

1/2 cup roasted pumpkin puree

1/2 teaspoon ground cinnamon

scant 1/8 teaspoon ground cloves

scant 1/8 teaspoon ground nutmeg

one recipe caramel sauce (p. 265) (optional)

1 cup sweetened whipped cream (optional)

TO PREPARE

Preheat the oven to 325°F degrees. In a large bowl, combine cream cheese, sugars, and maple syrup. Beat until smooth. Blend in eggs one at a time. Add pumpkin, cinnamon, cloves, and nutmeg to the batter and stir gently until well blended. Carefully pour the batter into the prepared crust. Bake for 35 minutes, or until the center is almost set. Allow to cool completely, then refrigerate for 4 hours or overnight.

FOR THE GARNISH

Cover generously with caramel sauce and swirl with whipped cream, if desired.

New York Cheesecake

This is the best way to take a bite out of the Big Apple, and the creamiest, most wonderful cheesecake recipe I have ever tasted. And trust me, I have tasted my share of cheesecake. Maybe your share too.

TO PREPARE

Mix graham crackers, butter, and 1/2 cup sugar together well and pat into the bottom and sides of a 9–10 inch springform pan. Put into the freezer while preparing the filling. Preheat the oven to 550°F degrees.

In a large bowl, mix the cream cheese, sugar, and flour until smooth and creamy. Add eggs, yolks, and vanilla—one at a time. Stir well between additions, scraping the sides of the bowl often.

Pour the filling over the crust. Wrap the bottom and halfway up the sides of pan with aluminum foil to prevent water seeping into the cheesecake. Place the cheesecake pan into a baking pan with sides and place into the oven. Fill the outer pan with hot water.

Bake at 550°F for 10–12 minutes or until puffed. If it starts turning brown too quickly, turn the oven down immediately. Reduce the oven to 200°F and bake for 1 hour or until the cake is mostly firm. The center will still jiggle slightly when the pan is shaken.

Remove from the oven and run a wet knife around edge to loosen. Cool on the countertop for 2 hours. Put in the refrigerator to cool completely overnight.

FOR THE GARNISH

Serve plain or with fruit topping drizzled over cheesecake, if desired.

FOR THE CRUST

15 full-size graham crackers (1 1/2 packages), crushed

1/2 cup melted butter

1/2 cup sugar

FILLING

5 (8-ounce) packages cream cheese, softened

1 3/4 cups sugar

3 tablespoons all-purpose flour

5 large eggs

2 large egg yolks

1/2 teaspoon vanilla extract

fruit topping (optional)

Angel Cream Pie

This delicate pie lets the bright flavor of pineapple shine, but the glossy meringue filling does its due by sprinkling in the right amount of breezy fluff.

One 9-inch baked pastry pie crust

1 ¼ cup sugar

¼ cup cornstarch

¼ teaspoon salt

2 cups boiling water

2 large egg whites

1 teaspoon vanilla

1 (15-ounce) can crushed pineapple

whipped cream (optional)

TO PREPARE

In a bowl, sift together the sugar, cornstarch, and salt. Add to boiling water and continue boiling for 5 minutes. Remove from heat and set aside to cool. Place egg whites in a bowl and beat until soft peaks form. Add the cooled sugar mixture to the egg whites and beat for 10 minutes. Add the vanilla and pineapple. Beat for an additional 10 minutes. Pour the mixture into the baked pie crust. Refrigerate for 4 hours or overnight before serving.

FOR THE GARNISH

Top with whipped cream, if desired.

Key Lime Pie

It's the tart lime juice that makes all the difference in a key lime pie, and this recipe's got juice. Landlubbers might add green food coloring, but purists like you and I know that an authentic key lime is as yellow as a newborn chick. Don't believe me? Try it au naturale and thank me later.

TO PREPARE

Preheat oven to 325°F. In a bowl blend the lime juice with the sweetened condensed milk. Add the sour cream and sugar. Add the beaten eggs to lime juice mixture; blend until fully incorporated. Pour the mixture into the prepared crust and bake for 15 minutes. Remove from the oven and let cool 1 hour.

FOR THE GARNISH

Top with sweetened whipped cream and garnish with lime twists and zest, if desired.

FOR THE CRUST

One pastry, shortbread, graham cracker, or gingersnap crust

INGREDIENTS

1 cup key lime juice

2 (14-ounce) cans sweetened condensed milk

1/2 cup sour cream

4 tablespoons sugar

2 large eggs, beaten

whipped cream (optional)

lime twists and zest (optional)

Tropical Storm Pie

Heaping dollops of whipped cream and maraschino cherries swirl around a storm's eye while pineapple macadamia nut filling lashes out at the drowning crust. Enter the maelstrom at your own risk.

FOR THE CRUST

One 9-inch graham cracker crust, baked for 10 minutes

INGREDIENTS

4 ounces cream cheese, softened

1/2 (14-ounce) can sweetened condensed milk

1/4 cup lemon juice

1/2 teaspoon vanilla extract

FOR THE TOPPING

1 banana

1/2 (20-ounce) can or 1 (8-ounce) can crushed pineapple, drained and reserve juice

1 recipe cherry pie filling (p. 99)

2 cups whipped topping (optional)

1/2 cup flaked coconut (optional)

1/2 cup macadamia nuts (optional)

maraschino cherries, about one dozen (optional)

TO PREPARE

With a mixer, beat the cream cheese until light and fluffy, about 3 minutes. Slowly add the sweetened condensed milk, mixing on low speed until well combined. Stir in the lemon juice and vanilla and pour into the crust. Place the pie into the refrigerator for at least 2 hours, until well chilled and set.

TO PREPARE

Slice the banana and place in bowl. Pour reserved pineapple juice over the bananas and let sit for 10 minutes to preserve the bananas and keep them from browning on the pie. After the bananas sit, drain and place bananas on cream cheese layer. Spread the pineapple over bananas. Next, spread the cherry pie filling on the pineapples.

FOR THE GARNISH

Decorate with the whipped topping. Sprinkle the coconut and macadamia nuts on top and decorate the edges with maraschino cherries, if desired.

Chapter Four

Fruit Pies

While light and fluffy cream pies traditionally anchor springtime and summer, in winter, the stove's warm glow makes the slow-baking of a luscious apple pie a quintessential part of any baker's life. The gentle aroma of cinnamon, nutmeg, and ginger are apt to give any ordinary day the feeling of Christmas. So while your hearth heats your home, let these pies scent the air, for nothing says *family* like a cherry pie. And when the days do grow hot again, don't fret: a quickly prepped rhubarb, blueberry, or peach pie placed out on a windowsill gives springtime enough motivation to keep coming around, year after year, for one more whiff of the truly sublime.

Apple Skillet Pie

The expression goes, "As American as apple pie," so go ahead, be a patriot. The skillet allows for an exceptionally crispy crust—a nice improvisation for a classic that never goes out of style.

FOR THE CRUST

One 9-inch unbaked pastry pie crust

INGREDIENTS

4 or more medium-sized cooking apples, such as Granny Smith

3 tablespoons maple syrup

2 heaping tablespoons all-purpose flour

1 cup sugar

3/4 cup warm water

2 tablespoons butter

1 teaspoon ground cinnamon

TO PREPARE

Preheat oven to 450°F. Peel, core, and slice apples. Place in a bowl and pour maple syrup over the apple slices. Place apple slices in the pie crust so that it's generously filled. In a bowl, stir flour, sugar, and warm water together until smooth. Pour over apple-filled pie crust. Dot with butter. Sprinkle cinnamon over apples. Bake at 450°F until the crust is browned. Reduce heat to 350°F and continue baking until apples are tender.

TIP: To create a beautiful pie, spiral cut the apples and place in circles around the pan, working inward.

Ground Cherry Pie

Both tart and sweet, ground cherries are often a forgotten fruit, a golden yellow outcast in the farmers' market. But with this pie, what once was lost, now is found—and that's one amazing ace up a baker's sleeve.

TO PREPARE

Simmer the cherries and 3 cups of water in a saucepan for 10 minutes over medium heat. In a small bowl, combine sugar, cornstarch and salt with just enough water to make a paste. Bring cherries to a boil over medium-high heat; add paste, stirring to incorporate thoroughly. Continue boiling for 30 seconds. Add vinegar and lemon. Stir and remove from heat. Let cool. Pour mixture into unbaked pie crust. Cover with top crust and seal. Be sure to score top for venting. Bake at 425° for 15 minutes. Reduce temperature to 350°F and continue baking for 25 minutes. Serve chilled.

FOR THE CRUST

Two 9-inch unbaked pastry pie crusts

INGREDIENTS

1 1/2 cups fresh ground cherries

3 cups water

3/4 cup sugar

1/4 cup cornstarch

1/4 teaspoon salt

1/2 teaspoon white vinegar

2 drops lemon extract or flavoring

Mixed Berry Pie

In the pie world, this versatile blend of tart blackberries, sweet strawberries, and juicy raspberries proves that diversity equals mouth-watering.

FOR THE CRUST

Two 9-inch unbaked pastry pie crusts

INGREDIENTS

3 cups mixed berries (blackberries, strawberries, raspberries, and/or blueberries)

1 1/2 cups water

1 1/4 cups sugar

1/4 cups cornstarch

1 tablespoon lemon juice

2 tablespoons butter

dash salt

dash of ground nutmeg

whipped cream (otional)

vanilla ice cream (optional)

TO PREPARE

Preheat the oven to 400°F. Mix berries with water, sugar, and cornstarch in a saucepan. Cook over medium heat until thick, stirring occasionally. Add lemon, butter, salt, and nutmeg. Remove from heat. Let cool in refrigerator 30 minutes. Pour into unbaked pie crust. Cover with top crust and seal. Score top crust to vent. Bake for 10 minutes at 400°F. Reduce heat to 350°F and continue baking for an additional 30 minutes.

FOR THE GARNISH

Serve with whipped cream or vanilla ice cream, if desired.

Apple Snitz Pie

A staple of after-church Amish potlucks for decades, this buttery helping of warm apple goodness gains a sharp flavor from the dried apples in its recipe. Snitz! (Gesundheit!)

TO PREPARE

Preheat the oven to 425°F. Place apples in water and soak. In a medium saucepan, cook the apples over low heat until soft. Mash the apples and add the lemon extract and brown sugar. Pour the mixture into an unbaked pie crust. Cover with the top crust. Seal the edges. Bake at 425°F for 15 minutes; then reduce heat to 350°F for an additional 30 minutes.

FOR THE GARNISH

Serve the pie warm, topped with whipped cream or vanilla ice cream, desired.

FOR THE CRUST

Two 9-inch unbaked pastry pie crusts

INGREDIENTS

3 cups dried apples

2 1/4 cups warm water

1 teaspoon lemon extract

2/3 cup firmly packed brown sugar

whipped cream (otional)

vanilla ice cream (optional)

Apple Sugar Plum Pie

This melodious recipe performs a pas de deux over the tongue like the Sugar Plum Fairy herself; use a tart plum variety for a nice balance of flavor, and don't forget the orange juice for that citrusy "grand battement"!

FOR THE CRUST

Two 9-inch unbaked pastry pie crusts

INGREDIENTS

1 pound plums (about 2 1/2 cups), pitted and quartered

1 pound apples (about 2 1/2 cups), peeled, cored, and cut into chunks

2 tablespoons sugar

1 tablespoon butter

1/8 teaspoon ground cinnamon

2 tablespoons orange juice

crystal or sanding sugar

whipped cream (otional)

vanilla ice cream (optional)

TO PREPARE

Preheat oven to 350°F. Place fruit in large bowl and sprinkle with sugar, butter, cinnamon, and orange juice. Fold gently to coat the fruit. Pour the mixture into an unbaked pie crust. Cover with top crust and seal. Score vents into top crust and sprinkle with sanding sugar. Bake for 40 minutes.

FOR THE GARNISH

Serve hot or cold with whipped cream or vanilla ice cream, if desired.

Concord Grape Pie

Concord grapes are called a "slip skin" variety because the skin is easily separated from the fruit. Unfortunately, this tangy delight isn't considered a "slip waist" variety, because it is not easily separated from a tightening belt.

TO PREPARE

Preheat oven to 450°F. Wash, drain, and stem grapes. Gently remove skins from the fruit. Set skins aside in a separate bowl. Simmer the pulp in a saucepan over medium heat for about 5 minutes. Carefully put the hot pulp through a sieve, making sure to remove all of the seeds. Add skins back to pulp. Add sugar and flour to grapes. Add the lemon and melted butter to grape mixture. Pour the mixture into the pie crust. Cover with top crust or crumbs. Bake at 450°F for 10 minutes, then reduce heat to 350°F. Continue baking for an additional 30 minutes.

FOR THE GARNISH

Serve cold with whipped cream or vanilla ice cream, if desired.

FOR THE CRUST

Two 9-inch unbaked pastry pie crusts or single bottom crust and crumb topping

INGREDIENTS

3 cups concord grapes

1 cup sugar

3 tablespoons all-purpose flour

1 tablespoon lemon juice

1 heaping tablespoon melted butter

whipped cream (optional)

vanilla ice cream (optional)

Strawberry Rhubarb Pie

Rhubarb's unique flavor lifts the homespun strawberry sweetness of this garden combo into new orbit, so hurry out to your local farm stand and pick up a few. Rhubarb season is short, but the experience of tasting this pie will last forever.

FOR THE CRUST

Two 9-inch unbaked pastry pie crusts

INGREDIENTS

4 cups chopped rhubarb, fresh (use only the red part of the plant; the green part is toxic)

2 1/2 cups strawberries, hulled and sliced

1/2 cup sugar

1/3 cup cornstarch

1 teaspoon lemon juice

egg wash

1/4 cup sanding sugar

whipped cream (otional)

vanilla ice cream (optional)

TO PREPARE

Preheat oven to 400°F. Sprinkle rhubarb and strawberries with sugar and cornstarch. Gently fold together with lemon juice until thoroughly coated. Pour fruit mixture into pie crust. Cover with top pastry crust. Score top with knife to allow pie to vent, or make a lattice crust. Brush crust with egg wash. Sprinkle with sanding sugar. Bake at 400°F for 15 minutes. Turn heat down to 300°F and continue baking for 1 hour. Loosely cover pie with parchment paper if crust browns too quickly.

FOR THE GARNISH

Serve well-chilled with whipped cream or a scoop of vanilla ice cream, if desired.

Red Raspberry Pie

There's no better mental image than a tart raspberry pie sitting on a checkered picnic blanket, so make your dream a reality with this piquant piece of pie perfection.

TO PREPARE

Preheat oven to 400°F. Cook raspberries with water, sugar, and cornstarch over medium heat until thick, stirring occasionally. Add lemon juice, butter, and salt. Remove from heat. Let mixture cool in the refrigerator 30 minutes. Pour cooled mixture into unbaked pie crust. Cover with top crust and seal. Score top crust to vent. Bake for 10 minutes at 400°F. Reduce heat to 350°F and continue baking for 30 minutes.

FOR THE GARNISH

Serve with whipped cream or vanilla ice cream, if desired.

FOR THE CRUST

Two 9-inch unbaked pastry pie crusts

INGREDIENTS

3 cups raspberries

1 1/4 cups water

1 cup sugar

1/4 cup cornstarch

1 tablespoon lemon juice

2 tablespoons butter

pinch of salt

whipped cream (otional)

vanilla ice cream (optional)

Blackberry Pie

A traditional dessert, blackberry pie takes flight on the freshness of its fruity namesake. So be an explorer, find a blackberry farm near you, and pick the best berries for yourself, because nothing tastes better than harvesting your own dessert!

FOR THE CRUST

Two 9-inch unbaked pastry pie crusts

INGREDIENTS

3 cups fresh or frozen blackberries

1 1/2 cups water

1 1/4 cups sugar

1/4 cup cornstarch

1 tablespoon lemon juice

2 tablespoons butter

dash salt

dash ground nutmeg

whipped cream (otional)

vanilla ice cream (optional)

TO PREPARE

Preheat the oven to 400°F. Mix blackberries with water, sugar, and cornstarch in a saucepan. Cook over medium heat until thick, stirring occasionally. Add lemon juice, butter, salt, and nutmeg. Remove from heat. Let cool in refrigerator 30 minutes. Pour into unbaked pie crust. Cover with top crust and seal. Score top crust to vent. Bake for 10 minutes at 400°F. Reduce heat to 350°F and continue baking for an additional 30 minutes.

FOR THE GARNISH

Serve with whipped cream or vanilla ice cream, if desired.

Cherry Pie

Of course I love all my pies equally, but there's only one I can sidle up next to any day and at any time, during any season and in any mood . . . Cherry, my BPFF (best pie friend forever).

TO PREPARE

Preheat oven to 400°F. Combine cherries with water, sugar, and cornstarch in a saucepan. Cook over medium heat until thick, stirring occasionally. Add butter and salt. Remove from heat. Add almond extract and vanilla. Let mixture cool in refrigerator for 30 minutes. Pour cooled mixture into unbaked pie crust. Cover with top crust and seal. Score top crust to vent. Bake for 10 minutes at 400°F. Reduce heat to 350°F and continue baking for 30 minutes.

FOR THE GARNISH

Serve with whipped cream or vanilla ice cream, if desired.

FOR THE CRUST

Two 9-inch unbaked pastry pie crusts

INGREDIENTS

4 cups fresh or frozen sweet cherries

1 1/4 cups water

1 cup sugar

1/4 cup cornstarch

2 tablespoons butter

1/4 teaspoon salt

1 teaspoon almond extract

1/2 teaspoon vanilla extract

whipped cream (otional)

vanilla ice cream (optional)

Sour Cherry Crunch Pie

Sour cherries are often called "wild cherries" for a reason—their unique and tart flavor can't be contained—and this recipe uses sour cherries to draw down sugary sweetness just enough to create a perfect blend of saucy saccharine simplicity.

FOR THE CRUST

One 9-inch unbaked pastry pie crust

INGREDIENTS

4 cups fresh or frozen sour cherries

1 1/4 cups water

1 cup sugar

1/4 cup cornstarch

2 tablespoons butter

1/4 teaspoon salt

1 teaspoon almond extract

1/2 teaspoon vanilla extract

crumb topping (p. 257–261)

whipped cream (otional)

vanilla ice cream (optional)

TO PREPARE

Preheat oven to 400°F. Combine cherries with water, sugar, and cornstarch in a saucepan. Cook over medium heat until thick, stirring occasionally. Add butter and salt. Remove from heat. Add the almond and vanilla extracts to the mixture. Let mixture cool in the refrigerator 30 minutes. Pour the cooled mixture into the unbaked pie crust.

FOR THE CRUMBS

Sprinkle your favorite crumb mixture over fruit filling. Bake for 10 minutes at 400°F. Reduce heat to 350°F and continue baking for 30 minutes.

FOR THE GARNISH

Serve with whipped cream or vanilla ice cream, if desired.

Cranberry Cherry Pie

Cran-apple and cran-grape juice drinks prove that cranberry works with any tasty fruit, and the comingling of sweet cherries and spiky cranberry flavor makes this recipe an interesting addition to any baker's toolbox.

TO PREPARE

Preheat oven to 375°F. In a bowl, mix sugar, flour, and vanilla. Stir in fruit. Spread coated fruit into bottom pie crust. Pour in cherry pie filling. Cover with top crust. Place in the freezer for 15 minutes. Remove from freezer, and brush top crust with cream or egg wash. Score crust to allow steam to vent. Sprinkle top with sanding sugar. Bake at 375°F for 60 minutes.

FOR THE GARNISH

Serve with whipped cream or vanilla ice cream, if desired.

FOR THE CRUST

Two 9-inch unbaked pastry pie crusts

INGREDIENTS

1 cup sugar

2 tablespoons all-purpose flour

1 teaspoon vanilla extract

2 cups cranberries, fresh or frozen

1 recipe cherry pie filling (p. 99)

cream or egg wash

1/4 cup sanding sugar

whipped cream (otional)

vanilla ice cream (optional)

Bodacious Blueberry Pie

Why bodacious? Well, Webster's *defines the word as "very good, impressive, and unmistakable," and blueberry pie is definitely those things, but the lemon peel/cinnamon double punch in this particular recipe is what satisfies* Webster's *second definition— "voluptuous." Just don't get caught staring.*

FOR THE CRUST

Two 9-inch unbaked
pastry pie crusts

INGREDIENTS

4 cups fresh
blueberries

3/4 cup sugar

3 tablespoons
cornstarch

1/4 teaspoon salt

1/2 teaspoon ground
cinnamon

dash ground nutmeg

1/4 teaspoon lemon zest

1 tablespoon butter

1 tablespoon sanding
sugar

whipped cream
(otional)

vanilla ice cream
(optional)

TO PREPARE

Preheat oven to 425°F. Wash blueberries and remove all stems. Pat berries dry with paper towels. Mix sugar, cornstarch, salt, cinnamon, and nutmeg together in bowl. Add lemon zest. Sprinkle mixture over blueberries. Gently fold mixture together and pour into unbaked pie crust. Top with butter. Cover pie with second crust by fluting the edges or making a lattice pattern. Sprinkle crust with sanding sugar. Bake at 425°F for 50 minutes, until the crust is golden brown. Let cool completely.

FOR THE GARNISH

Top with whipped cream or vanilla ice cream, if desired.

Skillet Pear Ginger Pie

This pie's crisp crust comes from the campfire cast-iron skillet, but the real dynamism behind this zesty surprise comes from the deft melding of hot ginger and sweet crunchy pear.

TO PREPARE

Preheat oven to 375°F. Lay one pie dough circle into a 10-inch cast-iron skillet. Slice pears and place in a large mixing bowl.

In a large bowl, mix together the flour, ginger, cinnamon, and sugars. Stir in lemon juice and cream. Add pear slices to mixture; toss to coat. Pour into pie crust. Cover fruit mixture with top layer vented pie dough, lattice crust, or other decorative designed crust. Brush dough with 1 egg yolk mixed with 3 tablespoons heavy cream.

Bake for 40 minutes at 375°F or until pear mixture is bubbling.

FOR THE GARNISH

Let cool enough to set and serve with vanilla ice cream, if desired. Caramel sauce drizzled over top makes an extra tempting treat! (See page 265 for recipe.)

FOR THE CRUST

Two 9-inch unbaked pastry pie crusts

INGREDIENTS

1/4 cup all-purpose flour

3/4 teaspoon ground ginger

1 teaspoon ground cinnamon

1/2 teaspoon salt

1/3 cup granulated sugar

1/3 cup firmly packed brown sugar

2 tablespoons freshly squeezed lemon juice

1 cup heavy cream

7–8 fresh bartlett pears, peeled and sliced

1 large egg yolk

3 tablespoons heavy cream

1 teaspoon light brown sugar

vanilla ice cream (optional)

caramel sauce (optional)

Peach Pie

This little number glistens like the Georgia sun that gives peaches life. Don't forget the tapioca, that deliciously fine native Brazilian starch, and make sure to enhance the intercontinental dance with a heaping scoop of cool vanilla ice cream.

FOR THE CRUST

Two 9-inch pastry pie crusts

INGREDIENTS

2 tablespoons cold butter, divided

2 tablespoons all-purpose flour

1 1/2 cups sugar

2 tablespoons minute tapioca

dash ground cinnamon

2 large eggs, beaten

3 cups fresh peaches, sliced

whipped cream (otional)

vanilla ice cream (optional)

TO PREPARE

Preheat oven to 450°F. Place 1 tablespoon butter and flour in bottom of unbaked pie crust. In a bowl, add sugar, tapioca, and cinnamon to beaten eggs mixture. Fold in peaches and pour into prepared pie crust. Cover with lattice crust and dot with remaining butter. Bake at 450°F for 15 minutes. Reduce heat to 350°F and continue baking for additional 25 minutes.

FOR THE GARNISH

This is delicious served with whipped cream or vanilla ice cream, if desired.

Fruit Slab Pie

Go big or go home. Use any fruit filling, doubled for your pleasure. Sanding sugar brushed over the crust gives the pie a candied tickle; the vanilla ice cream on the side brushes your palette with an icy sheen.

TO PREPARE

Preheat oven to 375°F. Roll out the dough and divide it in half. Press half of the dough into an 11 x 15-inch pan. Fill with the double recipe of fruit filling. Cover the filled pie with the top crust. Crimp the edges. Brush the top with egg wash and dust with sanding sugar. Score top with vents.

   Bake at 375°F for 1 hour. Let cool 30 minutes before serving.

FOR THE GARNISH

Serve warm with vanilla ice cream, if desired.

FOR THE CRUST

2 recipes double pastry pie crust

INGREDIENTS

Double recipe of your favorite fruit filling recipe

egg wash

1/4 cup sanding sugar

vanilla ice cream (optional)

A Slice of Amish Life: The Pie Contest

Attending a pie contest is like watching the Daytona 500 from the front seat of a 1976 Chevelle: you can see nirvana, but you can't taste it. But *judging* a pie contest? Well, that's different. Now you're behind the wheel.

"We should have a contest," I said to my friend Kjell.

We were sitting in the lobby of Everence Bank, a Mennonite-owned Pinecraft Institution. Kjell was the manager. We were trying to think of a new social event to add to the winter season calendar.

"What kind of contest?" he asked.

"I don't know," I said. But I did know.

He leaned back in his chair. "It probably on depends what kind of—"

"Pie," I blurted.

"Pie?"

I nodded firmly. "It has to be pie."

I was sure. Soon he was too, and the first Pinecraft Pie Contest was born.

Amish and Mennonite people vacation in Pinecraft between Thanksgiving and Easter. A friend of mine used to say, "When English people take a vacation to see Amish people, they visit Pennsylvania. But when Amish people take a vacation to see Amish people, they visit Pinecraft." She's right.

The winter season is a joyous affair for those traveling to Florida: it's a welcome respite from difficult farm life, and a chance to see friends and family living outside the range of a horse and buggy.

Starting around Thanksgiving, Plain people rush down from the North on charter buses; the buses start way up in Canada and head straight south, grabbing as many Amish and Mennonites as each one can hold. Whole families travel together.

Pinecraft is a madhouse henceforth. Good luck driving the streets after the buses arrive: hundreds of chatty Amish women blockade you from curb to curb. Good luck visiting the park or the restaurants: you're hemmed in by plain dresses, long beards, and toothy grins.

Over time, the idle neighboring grew into a set of annual social events that many people now look forward to all year long. These events—the Haiti Auction and the Christmas Day Parade—have long since become tradition, each with their own mystique.

Kjell and I had met at the bank because we felt it was time for a new tradition.

I asked him, "I wonder what pie I should make?"

"Make?" he said. "Sherry, you won't be making any pies."

"Why not?"

"Well, you'd be a judge, of course."

Oh my, I thought. *This is going to be fun.*

Leading up to the contest, let's just say I fasted on nothing but iceberg let-tuce and water for two days. Let's say that, because it was really four days.

I was an amateur turning pro. And I was going to be ready.

We'd chosen the bank parking lot for the pie contest. Organizers roped off the space and covered the judging area in a food tent to ward off the hot sun. Reporters steadily trickled in. It was Sarasota's mini ver-sion of the Nathan's Hot Dog Eating Contest—but not gross.

I picked a bouquet of flowers from my garden and arranged them in the front basket of my bicycle. The bank is a half mile from my house. The route weaves through cheery camper homes and freshly painted one-room cottages. It takes five minutes to pedal.

When I arrived at the bank, Kjell gave me a judge's badge right away; the contest was set to begin. But something seemed very wrong from the start. What was it? The crowd was excited. The presentation looked professional. What seemed so . . . off?

"Oh no," I gasped.

It was the pies. We'd planned on roughly twenty-five entries. But there, on the wonderfully decorated contestant table, were a measly six.

Six! The contest had three pie categories, each with 1st, 2nd, and 3rd place prizes: that's nine winners, and we didn't even have nine pies.

This was a major disaster. What happened? At least twenty of my friends had intended to enter the contest. Why had so few actually done it?

I had to get some answers, and fast. So I approached Fannie, a trusted friend. She knew everything about Pinecraft.

"Fannie, what happened?!" I asked her.

"What do you mean?" she said.

"There are no pies!"

Her eyes darkened. "Oh no." She looked to the table and covered her mouth. "Oh, they didn't bring them over, I bet."

"Who?" I asked.

"Everybody."

That's when it hit me: modesty. All those lovely Amish women, who'd spent all morning baking their best pies, each of them thrilled to do so, had finished up, wiped their hands with delight, and suddenly frowned.

I could see it in my mind's eye: "Who am I to enter a contest?" each one said in chorus, twenty women separated by space but not temperament. "I should let others enjoy this year, and I'll try the next."

And then every one of those lovely ladies placed their cherished pies down on the counter and marched right out of the house.

They all stood before me now. A Spartan army who'd left their spears at home.

I turned back to Fannie. "You have to help me. We have to tell everyone to get their pies!"

"Ok!" she said, as I turned away. "But, Sherry?"

I glanced back. "Yes?"

"Should I get mine too?"

"Yes! Yes, Fannie!" I spun her toward her house. "Go and get it. I'll tell the rest."

Her face lit up like the underside of a space shuttle, and she was off just as quick. I went person to person, asking my friends if they had made a pie.

"Yes," most of them said.

"Well . . ." I hesitated. "Don't you think you could maybe bring it over and enter the contest?"

"I guess I could," each said but still didn't move.

"Could you please get your pie?" I insisted. "For me?"

That was it. "Yes," each one said and raced off.

Word traveled fast. The women traveled fast, too, because ten minutes later we had twenty-five entries ready to go. The cavalry had arrived, led by General Custard herself.

❖

The rules were simple: contestants must live in Sarasota and must have made his or her own pie. We were shocked when one lady entered a chocolate pie from a supermarket bakery, still in its plastic container. I didn't want to humiliate her, but I didn't want her to win either, so I put her pie off to the side.

Ultimately, it didn't matter anyway—that pie tasted so bad, I lost weight eating it.

My seat was closest to the pies. Twenty-five luscious, homemade treats. And one from Publix. My nose followed each one indiscriminately. I wanted to go where *that* pie was going . . . but then there'd be another, and I'd forget about the first. It was like young love.

We began by sampling two bites from each pie and a drink of water afterward. Those tastes! Each fruit pie was a full springtime. Each cream pie a frothy dream. Every one offered something different, something I'd never tasted before.

A short list of the highlights:

- Blueberry pie: so presumptuous and so beautiful. It tasted high-end. Well-bred and upscale, like a Vanderbilt.
- Peach and cherry, the old maids. They knew who they were; they'd been around forever. There was nothing left to prove.
- Orange pie: this is the pie I want in heaven.
- Custard: It jiggled! Reminded me of Marilyn Monroe. Did it just wink at me?
- Montgomery pie: a stranger. It slipped onto the table, tasted great, and then slipped out again unnoticed. What was that masked taste? Will I ever see it again?
- Raspberry cream . . . oh, you devil. Rich and thin—and thin is always in. I didn't know that flavor of decadence existed.
- Lemon pie: It wouldn't quit, like a freckle-faced girl from the neighborhood, a chatty Kathy who stops her bike out front while you're gardening to talk ten minutes without a breath about boys, boys, and gossip. My mouth was a lemon for ten minutes. It wouldn't go away.
- Chocolate cream pie: an unexpected explosion. Like sitting down next to a clump of trees on the night of July 4th, only to realize those "trees" are the firework cannons. BOOM.

- Apple pie. I didn't like apple pie; the crust told me why: "You haven't met the right one." I blanked out. Where was I? Oh, at the pie contest. That apple pie should be prescription only.

There were so many rich pies, one of the judges got groggy and had to take a break, get some coffee. I powered through. I was born for this.

Scores were totaled, and the raspberry cream pie swept all three categories—taste, appearance, and overall—in the "Best Cream Pie" competition. The same baker won "Best Fruit Pie" and "Best One Crust Pie" too. She got three identical first-place prize baskets. It was an epic sweep.

After the prizes, we ended the contest by treating everyone to free pie and a chili lunch. Quite a few people approached me to ask how I had become one of the judges. Some were casual about it, using the question as a way of starting conversation. But others had jealousy in their eyes. They wanted a place at that table.

A week later I had Kjell nail a brass plaque to a small foldout chair. The plaque read "Sherry Gore, Pie Judge." Now it's official.

Nobody is taking that seat away from me.

Chapter Five

One Crust Pies

*Most pies aren't comfortable unless they're cov-*ered in crust completely, but these immodest sweet tooth suitors have the joie de vivre to make a splash on any dessert tray by baring it all. From lemon meringue to double chocolate to marshmallow brownie to cream cheese pecan, make one of these sartorial showoffs and whip your guests into a frenzy, because this batch erupts in flavor from the first bite. It has been said, "If you've got it, flaunt it," and a smart baker knows that one crust pies can really draw a crowd. So when your guests are looking for a bit of brassy fun, take the top down, rev these convertibles, and don't be afraid to let them strut their stuff(ing).

Lemon Sponge Pie

This recipe calls for the "juice and grated zest of one lemon," and frankly, that sentence alone should be enough to call this dessert into service. The baked egg whites give air to the light sponge filling—a frivolous mélange of citrus charm.

TO PREPARE

Preheat oven to 350°F. In a bowl, cream butter, sugar, flour, and egg yolks; beat well. Add salt, lemon juice and zest, and hot water. In a separate bowl, beat egg whites until stiff. Fold into mixture. Pour into unbaked pie crust. Bake at 350°F for 45 minutes, or until set.

FOR THE GARNISH

Top with whipped cream and sliced lemon, if desired.

FOR THE CRUST

One 9-inch unbaked pastry pie crust

INGREDIENTS

2 tablespoons butter, softened

1 cup sugar

3 tablespoons all-purpose flour

3 large eggs, separated

1/2 teaspoon salt

juice and grated zest of one lemon

1 1/2 cups hot water

whipped cream (otional)

sliced lemon (optional)

Lemon Meringue Pie

A nimbus cloud sitting atop a gilded throne; a snowcapped amber peak: the image of a classic lemon meringue slice calls no small amount of illusions to mind, and no small amount of portions to mouth. Careful with this lucent dream—you might wake up finding an empty pie plate.

FOR THE CRUST

One 9-inch baked pastry pie crust

INGREDIENTS

2 cups water

1 cup sugar

1/4 cup cornstarch

dash salt

1/3 cup lemon juice

3 large egg yolks

1 tablespoon butter

lemon zest (optional)

TO PREPARE

Bring water to a boil in a saucepan. Mix sugar, cornstarch, and salt together in a bowl. Stir in lemon juice. Add egg yolks and mix well. Stir mixture into water and return to a boil, stirring constantly. Remove from heat; add butter and let cool. Pour into baked crust. Top with the meringue.

FOR THE GARNISH

Grate fresh lemon zest over the pie for an extra citrus zing, if desired.

Luscious Lemon Pie

Creamier than its meringue sisters, luscious lemon adds sour cream to its medley for a unique texture more milky mousse than most, and more mouthwatering than many. Magnificent.

TO PREPARE

In the top of a double boiler, combine sugar, cornstarch, and salt. Stir in egg yolks, milk, and lemon juice. Cook and stir for 3 minutes. Remove from heat and stir in butter and lemon zest. Cool, stirring occasionally. When mixture reaches room temperature, stir in sour cream. Pour into pie crust and refrigerate overnight.

FOR THE GARNISH

Top with whipped cream, if desired.

FOR THE CRUST

One 9-inch baked pastry pie crust

INGREDIENTS

1 cup sugar

3 tablespoons cornstarch

dash salt

3 large egg yolks, slightly beaten

1 cup milk

1/3 cup lemon juice

1/4 cup butter

grated zest from 1 lemon

1 cup sour cream

whipped cream (optional)

Lemon Icebox Pie

Give this quick and easy lemon tart a heavy cream bonnet and graham cracke. bangs, and then sit back and wait for your guests to ask which bakery you bought it from.

FOR THE CRUST

One 9-inch prepared graham cracker crust

INGREDIENTS

2 (14-ounce) cans sweetened condensed milk

1 cup freshly squeezed lemon juice

6 large egg yolks, beaten

1 cup heavy cream

1 cup sour cream

2 tablespoons confectioners' sugar

lemon slices

TO PREPARE

Preheat oven to 350°F. Combine sweetened condensed milk and lemon juice with egg yolks and beat. Pour into prepared crust. Bake at 350°F for 15 minutes. Let cool completely, then transfer to the refrigerator to chill overnight.

FOR THE GARNISH

Combine heavy cream, sour cream, and confectioners' sugar and whip until fluffy. Spoon over pie. Top with lemon slices. Serve chilled.

Frozen Pink Lemonade Pie

Pink lemonade has an awfully "shady" history: beach umbrellas, patio enclosures, mid-day parasols, and oak tree canopies on hot summer days. So let this white-picket-fence slice of Americana join the ranks and send a fresh breeze through the hottest afternoons.

TO PREPARE

In the bowl of an electric mixer, beat cream cheese and sweetened milk together. Add concentrate and lemon juice. Add food coloring, a couple of drops at a time, until desired color is achieved. Pour filling into prepared graham cracker crust. Freeze until firm. Let thaw on counter 15 minutes before serving.

FOR THE GARNISH

Top with whipped cream, if desired.

FOR THE CRUST

One 9-inch prepared graham cracker crust

INGREDIENTS

1 (8-ounce) package cream cheese, softened

1 (14-ounce) can sweetened condensed milk

3/4 cup pink lemonade concentrate (do not dilute)

2 tablespoons lemon juice

red food coloring

whipped cream (optional)

Frozen Pumpkin Pie

An unexpectedly cool twist on a classic autumnal recipe, frozen pumpkin pie is so cool it never breaks a sweat (because it won't last long enough on your dessert tray to do so).

FOR THE CRUST

One 9-inch baked graham cracker crust

INGREDIENTS

1 cup pumpkin puree (see recipe on p. 136 for roasted pumpkin)

1/2 cup sugar

1/2 teaspoon salt

1/2 teaspoon ground nutmeg

1/2 teaspoon ground cinnamon

1/8 teaspoon allspice

1 quart vanilla ice cream

whipped cream (optional)

FOR THE FILLING

In a bowl, combine pumpkin, sugar, nutmeg, cinnamon, and allspice. Fold in the ice cream until thoroughly incorporated. Pour into baked graham cracker crust. Freeze at least 4 hours.

FOR THE GARNISH

Serve plain or with a dollop of whipped cream, if desired.

Sue Mullet's Famous Pumpkin Pie

Sue isn't famous but her recipe sure is, a perfect distillation of time-honored ingredients with a vivacious dash of clove. Make a reputation of your own at holiday dinners serving this antique indulgence, but make sure to give Sue her due. She's earned it.

TO PREPARE

Preheat oven to 425°F. Mix sugar, salt, cinnamon, ginger, and cloves in small bowl. Set aside. In a large bowl, beat eggs. Stir in pumpkin and spice mixture. Gradually add evaporated milk, combining thoroughly. Pour mixture into pie crust. Bake at 425°F for 15 minutes, then reduce heat to 350°F and continue baking for additional 45 minutes. Let cool completely before serving.

FOR THE GARNISH

Serve plain or decorate top with dollops of whipped cream, if desired.

FOR THE CRUST

One 9-inch unbaked pastry pie crust

INGREDIENTS

3/4 cup sugar

1/2 teaspoon salt

1 teaspoon ground cinnamon

1/2 teaspoon ground ginger

1/4 teaspoon ground cloves

2 large eggs

2 cups pumpkin puree (p. 136)

1 (12-ounce) can evaporated milk

whipped cream (optional)

Roasted Pumpkin Puree

I say the most important part of any good pumpkin pie is its puree. It seems like common sense, I know, but it's true. The taste you get from roasting your own pumpkin is so much better than anything that plops out of a can. These instructions will put you on your way to an award-winning dessert.

To make your own pumpkin puree, which has a taste unlike anything you can get in a can, purchase pie pumpkins at your local market. These are readily available each fall.

Because the outer layer of pie pumpkins is far thicker than that of carving pumpkins, you'll want to roast them first. Simply place them whole on a heavy-duty baking sheet and roast at 350°F for about 20 minutes. Once they've cooled, use a serrated knife to cut each pumpkin in quarters. Scoop out the seeds and rind. Seeds may be saved for roasting later. Discard the rind.

Using the same baking sheet, place the pumpkin pieces side by side, skin side up. Roast for 45 minutes at 350°F. Remove from the oven and let cool. Using an ice-cream scoop or heavy spoon, scoop the pumpkin from the shells. Mash with a fork, potato masher, or use an electric mixer to cream the pumpkin.

Puree may be frozen or used immediately for your favorite recipes calling for pumpkin.

Congealed

Beef

CASSEROLES

Chicken

Cookies

Cake Icings

Yeast Bread

Bisc

2.

Prune Cake

13. Spice Cake

½ cup shortening (butter or

Sweet Potato Pie

My son told me that he disliked sweet potatoes, so I made him this pie. Never heard that from him again.

FOR THE CRUST

One 9-inch unbaked pastry pie crust

INGREDIENTS

1/3 cup butter

1/2 cup firmly packed brown sugar

2 large eggs, beaten

3/4 cup heavy cream

2 cups sweet potato, cooked and mashed

1 teaspoon vanilla extract

1/2 teaspoon ground cinnamon

1/4 teaspoon ground ginger

1/4 teaspoon salt

dash ground nutmeg (optional)

whipped cream (optional)

TO PREPARE

Preheat oven to 425°F. Mix all ingredients together thoroughly in a bowl. Pour into the pie crust. Bake at 425°F for 15 minutes. Reduce heat to 350°F and continue baking for 40 minutes, being careful not to burn the crust. Remove from the oven and let cool. Refrigerate until ready to serve.

FOR THE GARNISH

Top with 1 cup sweetened whipped cream and a dash of nutmeg, if desired.

Pie Shoppe Caramel Pie

This easy-breezy dulce de leche looks like it came out of a 1950's soda shop and tastes like your sweetest memory. So pull up a stool and have some fun decorating a little slice of future nostalgia.

TO PREPARE

Spread caramel in prepared, cooled crust.

FOR THE GARNISH

Decorate with halo of whipped topping. Sprinkle with pecans and chocolate chips, if desired.

FOR THE CRUST

One 9-inch baked graham cracker crust

INGREDIENTS

2 (7-ounce) cans prepared caramel

whipped topping (optional)

1/3 cup chopped pecans (optional)

1/3 cup semisweet mini chocolate chip morsels (optional)

Classic Caramel Pie

This made-from-scratch recipe gives you full ownership of a confectionery classic, the caramel pie, and lets you finally use that candy thermometer up in the cupboard.

One 9-inch baked pastry or graham cracker crust

FOR THE FILLING

3/4 cup sugar

3/4 cup firmly packed brown sugar

6 tablespoons butter

1/2 cup half-and-half or heavy cream

3 tablespoons cornstarch

3/4 cup light corn syrup

1 tablespoon vanilla extract

2 cups whipped topping (optional)

1/3 cup chopped pecans (optional)

semisweet chocolate shavings (optional)

TO PREPARE

Mix the sugars, butter, half-and-half, cornstarch, and corn syrup in a heavy-bottomed saucepan. Gently heat on medium-low, stirring often, until the sugars are dissolved and the mixture reaches a low boil, reaching 250°F on a candy thermometer. Remove from heat, add vanilla, and beat with a wooden spoon until the mixture is creamy and smooth, then pour into a pastry crust or, if you're using a graham cracker crust, allow it to cool for 15 minutes before pouring in. Chill for 2–3 hours before topping.

FOR THE GARNISH

Decorate with whipped topping or whipped cream. Sprinkle with pecans and chocolate shavings, if desired.

Butterscotch Pie

Any pie featuring this homemade confectionery joy—made up of brown sugar, cream, vanilla, and butter—will linger on the tongue well after the dishes are put away and the lights turned low. Sweet, sweet dreams.

TO PREPARE

Brown butter in a saucepan over low heat. Add brown sugar and hot water, being careful as it may spatter. In a separate bowl, blend egg yolks, flour, evaporated milk, salt, and cornstarch with whisk or in a blender. Add milk mixture slowly and carefully to hot sugar mixture. Cook over medium heat until thick, stirring constantly. Remove from heat; add vanilla. Pour into crust and refrigerate until ready to serve.

FOR THE GARNISH

Top with meringue or whipped cream, if desired.

FOR THE CRUST

One 9-inch baked pastry pie crust

INGREDIENTS

2 tablespoons butter

1 cup firmly packed brown sugar

1/2 cup hot water

2 large egg yolks

2 tablespoons all-purpose flour

2 cups evaporated milk

1 teaspoon salt

3 tablespoons cornstarch

1 teaspoon vanilla extract

meringue (optional)

whipped cream (optional)

Cream Cheese Pecan Pie

Pecans and cream cheese, two Southern favorites that please palates across the globe, give this recipe a brilliant dash of homespun hospitality. Sprinkle the crust with confectioners' sugar for a messy, artful look, and a reminder of how funnel cakes got so popular at state fairs.

FOR THE CRUST

One 9-inch unbaked pastry pie crust

INGREDIENTS

1 (8-ounce) package cream cheese, softened

1 large egg, beaten

1/2 cup sugar

1 teaspoon vanilla extract

1/2 teaspoon salt

1 1/2 cups chopped pecans

FOR THE TOPPING

3 eggs

1/2 teaspoon vanilla extract

1 cup light corn syrup

vanilla ice cream (optional)

FOR THE FILLING

In a large bowl, cream together the cream cheese, egg, sugar, vanilla, and salt. Spread the mixture into the bottom of the pie crust. Sprinkle with pecan pieces.

Combine all topping ingredients and beat well. Bake at 375°F for 35–40 minutes, until topping is golden brown.

FOR THE GARNISH

Serve cold or warm with a scoop of vanilla ice cream, if desired.

Pecan Pie

The pecan resembles the Southern belle: elegant, alluring, and a bit mysterious. This recipe doesn't hold back the charm either—"I do declare." (Flutters paper fan in front of face)

TO PREPARE

Preheat oven to 350°F. Mix eggs, sugar, butter, salt, corn syrup, and vanilla in a bowl. Stir in chopped pecans. Pour into pie crust. Reserve 1/4 cup of filling. Top with pecan halves. Pour reserved filling over the top of the crust. Bake at 350°F for 60–70 minutes.

FOR THE GARNISH

Serve with vanilla ice cream, if desired.

TIP: To create the elegant look pictured here, top the pie filling with whole pecans, starting at the edge of the pie and working your way inward with the pecans.

FOR THE CRUST

One 9-inch unbaked pastry pie crust

INGREDIENTS

3 large eggs, beaten

1/2 cup firmly packed brown sugar

1/3 cup butter, melted

1/2 teaspoon salt

1 cup light corn syrup

1 teaspoon vanilla extract

1/2 cup chopped pecans

1 cup pecan halves

vanilla ice cream (optional)

White Chocolate Macadamia Nut Pie

There are two kinds of people in the world: those who like macadamia nuts and those who don't. If you're the latter, this recipe, with its daffy swirl of white chocolate, almond, and vanilla potpourri, gives you the best chance to change your mind.

FOR THE CRUST

One 9-inch baked pastry pie crust

INGREDIENTS

1/2 cup all-purpose flour

dash salt

1/2 cup sugar

1/2 cup firmly packed brown sugar

1 1/2 sticks butter, softened

1 teaspoon vanilla extract

1/2 teaspoon almond extract

2 large eggs

1 cup white chocolate chips, plus extra for topping

1 cup chopped macadamia nuts

whipped cream (optional)

TO PREPARE

Preheat oven to 325° F. In a large bowl, mix the flour, salt, white sugar and brown sugar. Blend in the butter, vanilla, almond extract, and eggs. Stir in the white chocolate chips and macadamia nuts. Pour the batter into the pie crust. Bake for 45–60 minutes at 325°F.

FOR THE GARNISH

Drizzle cooled pie with melted white chocolate or top with a little whipped cream and white chocolate chips, if desired.

German Chocolate Pie

Viele Köche verderben den Brei (too many cooks spoil the broth), so make sure to fly solo when baking this fraulein's feast, a pie version of German chocolate cake that will send your Pennsylvania Dutch friends over the moon.

TO PREPARE

Preheat oven to 450°F. Melt chocolate and butter in double boiler. In a separate saucepan, mix sugar and cornstarch together. Whisk in evaporated milk. Cook over low heat and stir until thickened. Place the egg in a small bowl and whisk in a small amount of hot milk mixture. Return to pan. Stir in the salt and vanilla and let cool. Slowly pour chocolate and milk mixture into unbaked pie crust. Sprinkle nuts and coconut on top. Sprinkle nuts and coconut flakes into unbaked pie crust. Bake at 450°F for 12 minutes. Reduce oven temperature to 350°F and continue baking for 20 minutes. Chill in refrigerator for several hours before serving.

FOR THE CRUST

One 9-inch unbaked pastry pie crust

INGREDIENTS

1 ounce German chocolate

1/4 cup butter

1 cup sugar

2 tablespoons cornstarch

1 1/2 cups evaporated milk

1 large egg

1/8 teaspoon salt

1/2 teaspoon vanilla extract

3/4 cup chopped pecans

1 cup flaked coconut

Double Chocolate Chess Pie

In dessert making, chocolate is always the answer. Who cares what the question is?

One 9-inch unbaked chocolate cookie pie crust

5 tablespoons cocoa powder, divided

1 1/2 cups sugar

1/4 teaspoon salt

3 tablespoons all-purpose flour

1 1/2 sticks butter

2 tablespoons vanilla extract

1 tablespoon cocoa powder

4 large eggs, lightly beaten

Preheat oven to 350°F. Bake crust for 7–10 minutes. Mix 4 tablespoons cocoa, sugar, salt, and flour in a bowl. Melt butter in microwave and add to cocoa mixture. Add vanilla and remaining cocoa powder. Beat in the eggs. Pour into the pie crust and bake at 350°F for 45 minutes.

Go-for-Broke Brownie Pie

This brown-eyed girl wins big either as a whole pie or a set of petite singles—if it ain't broke, don't fix it.

TO PREPARE

Preheat oven to 350°F. In a large bowl, cream butter and sugar. Add eggs and beat together. Add flour, vanilla, and salt. Fold in nuts last. Pour mixture into unbaked pie crust. Bake for 30 minutes. Remove from oven and immediately top with 2 cups of miniature marshmallows. Return to oven and bake for 5 more minutes. Remove from oven.

TO PREPARE CHOCOLATE FROSTING

Mix all ingredients together in a bowl and whisk until smooth. Using a rubber spatula, spread over melted marshmallow topped pie immediately after removing from oven.

FOR THE CRUST

One 9-inch unbaked chocolate pastry pie crust

FOR THE FILLING

1 cup butter, softened

3 cups sugar

5 large eggs

1 1/2 cups all-purpose flour

1 teaspoon vanilla extract

1 teaspoon salt

2 cups chopped nuts

2 cups miniature marshmallows

CHOCOLATE FROSTING

1/4 cup butter, softened

1/4 cup cocoa powder

1/4 cup heavy cream

1 cup confectioners' sugar

Chocolate Marshmallow Pie

With just four ingredients, this simple recipe is perfect for the harried mom. Of course, three of the four ingredients are chocolate, marshmallow, and whipped cream, so expect your kids to literally bounce off the walls afterward. I suggest buying a net.

FOR THE CRUST

One 9-inch baked chocolate cookie or one 9-inch baked pastry crust

INGREDIENTS

30 large marshmallows

3 ounces semisweet or milk chocolate

1/2 cup milk

1 cup whipped cream

1 cup whipped cream (optional)

chocolate shavings (optional)

TO PREPARE

Heat marshmallows, chocolate, and milk in double boiler until melted. Remove from heat; cool. When mixture has cooled, fold in 1 cup whipped cream. Pour into baked pie crust. Refrigerate until ready to serve.

FOR THE GARNISH

Top with whipped cream and chocolate shavings, if desired.

Peanut Butter Cup Pie

Who said monogamy was old fashioned? The union of peanut butter and chocolate changed my life, so let's support their marriage by inviting this scrumptious family of sugar, eggs, peanut butter, vanilla, and cocoa into our homes and our hearts.

FOR THE FILLING

Preheat oven to 350°F. In large bowl, mix together sugar, brown sugar, flour, cocoa powder, and salt. Add melted butter, vanilla, and peanut butter, and mix well. Next add the eggs and mix well. Finally, fold in the peanut butter cups and bake for 45 minutes at 350°F.

FOR THE GARNISH

When the pie is cooled, melt 1/4 cup milk chocolate chips and 1/4 cup peanut butter chips and drizzle on top of the pie, if desired.

SERVING SUGGESTION

This pie is so rich and decadent that it works well cut into small pieces, perfect for any occasion.

FOR THE CRUST

One 9-inch baked pastry pie crust

INGREDIENTS

1/2 cup white sugar

1/2 cup firmly packed brown sugar

1/4 cup all-purpose flour

1/4 plus 1/8 cup cocoa powder

dash salt

1 1/2 sticks butter, melted

1 teaspoon vanilla extract

2 tablespoons peanut butter

2 large eggs

22 mini peanut butter cups, cut in half

1/4 cup mini peanut butter cups (optional)

1/4 cup milk chocolate chips (optional)

Chapter Six

Traditional Pies

Try to picture the scene: a young Amish girl, not more than two years old, stands knee-high at her mother's apron on a panel-wood floor. The stove kettle hisses at the pot bubbling over with a baker's brew, caramel or homemade chocolate. Footsteps troll over the two room white-board house, a hive of activity. And the mother, her roller deep in cookie crust, her hands covered with flour, hums an organic hymn to herself as her dessert comes to life.

These pies are baked deep into young girls' own memories. Generation to generation, they are passed along, secret gifts to be re-gifted again. They are rolling treasure of accumulated experience—accumulated tradition—linking past, present, and future for all who take part. Join in, and remember.

Custard Pie

This recipe is from my bishop's wife—she won second place with this recipe. (This is the pie that jiggled when passed around!)

TO PREPARE

Preheat oven to 400°F. In a bowl, beat cream cheese and sugar together. Add eggs one at a time and beat well after each edition. Heat sweetened condensed milk, salt, and vanilla in a saucepan over medium heat until well combined. Beat until very foamy and pour into unbaked pie crust. Sprinkle with nutmeg. Bake 10 minutes. Reduce heat to 350°F and bake 25 minutes more or until done.

FOR THE GARNISH

Serve plain or with whipped cream, and grated nutmeg sprinkled on top, if desired.

FOR THE CRUST

One 9-inch unbaked pastry pie crust

INGREDIENTS

4 ounces cream cheese, softened

3/4 cup sugar

4 large eggs

2 cups milk

1/2 cup sweetened condensed milk

pinch salt

1 teaspoon vanilla extract

nutmeg, grated (optional)

whipped cream (optional)

Shoo-Fly Pie

Originally created to shoo pests away, this molasses-based pie was quickly crowned Lancaster, Pennsylvania's, beloved "Miss Popularity" for its reputation of becoming a social icon. This pie goes best with a strong cup of coffee and a circle of your family and friends.

FOR THE CRUST

One 9-inch unbaked pastry pie crust

INGREDIENTS

1 cup all-purpose flour

2/3 cup firmly packed brown sugar

1 tablespoon butter

1 teaspoon baking soda

3/4 cup hot water

1 cup molasses

1 large egg

whipped cream (optional)

TO PREPARE

Preheat oven to 400°F. In a bowl, mix together flour, brown sugar, and butter with a fork until crumbly. Measure out half the crumbs and set aside. In a separate bowl, dissolve baking soda in hot water. Add molasses and egg, then stir in half the crumbs. Pour mixture into unbaked pie crust. Top with remaining crumbs. Bake at 400°F for 10 minutes. Reduce heat to 325°F and continue baking for an additional 30 minutes.

FOR THE GARNISH

Serve with whipped cream, if desired.

Amish Vanilla Crumb Pie

Delicious served warm or cold, this traditional pie has earned its own star on the Amish Walk of Fame in Plain communities everywhere.

TO PREPARE

Preheat oven to 350°F. Combine brown sugar, flour, corn syrup, vanilla, and egg in a 2-quart saucepan. Slowly stir in water and cook over medium heat, stirring until mixture begins to boil. Remove from heat and let cool.

TO MAKE CRUMBS

In a large bowl mix together flour, baking soda, brown sugar, salt, cream of tartar, and butter until crumbly in texture. Pour cooled pie mixture into pie crust and top with crumbs. Bake for 40 minutes at 350°F, or until golden brown.

FOR THE GARNISH

Serve as it is or drizzle caramel sauce over top before serving, if desired. (See page 265 for recipe.)

FOR THE CRUST

One 9-inch unbaked pastry pie crust

INGREDIENTS

1/2 cup firmly packed brown sugar

1 tablespoon all-purpose flour

1/4 cup dark corn syrup

1 1/2 teaspoons vanilla extract

1 large egg, beaten

1 cup water

FOR THE CRUMBS

1 cup all-purpose flour

1/2 teaspoon baking soda

1/2 cup firmly packed brown sugar

1/8 teaspoon salt

1/2 teaspoon cream of tartar

1/4 cup butter, melted

caramel sauce (optional)

Bob Andy Pie

Amish folklore tells that an Amish farmer proclaimed this pie to be as good as his two favorite workhorses, Bob and Andy. The cloves and cinnamon give the pie a warm and spicy flavor for a taste as unique as its name.

FOR THE CRUST

One 9-inch unbaked pastry pie crust

INGREDIENTS

1 cup firmly packed brown sugar

2 tablespoons all-purpose flour

1/4 teaspoon ground cloves

1/2 teaspoon ground cinnamon

1 1/2 tablespoons butter, melted

2 large eggs, separated

1 cup milk

TO PREPARE

In a large bowl, mix together the brown sugar, flour, cloves, and cinnamon. Then add butter, egg yolks, and milk to the mixture. In a separate bowl, beat egg whites until stiff, then add to the milk mixture. Pour into unbaked pie crust. Bake at 400°F for 10 minutes. Reduce heat to 350°F and continue baking for 20–25 minutes, until the pie is set.

Union Pie

I love this pie! Made with sour cream, buttermilk, and dark molasses, this custard confidently charges in like a brisk cup of licorice coffee to preserve the harmony between your fork and your sweet tooth. United we stand, indeed.

TO PREPARE

Preheat oven to 400°F. In a bowl, combine sour cream, buttermilk, molasses, and egg. In a separate bowl, combine flour, baking soda, cinnamon, and nutmeg. Pour the flour mixture into the sour cream mixture and combine thoroughly. Pour the mixture into the unbaked pie crust. Bake at 400°F for 10 minutes. Reduce heat to 350°F and continue baking for 20–25 minutes, until a knife inserted into the center comes out clean.

FOR THE CRUST

One 9-inch unbaked pastry pie crust

INGREDIENTS

1/2 cup sour cream

1/2 cup buttermilk (or sour milk)

1/2 cup molasses

1 large egg, beaten

1/2 cup sugar

1 tablespoon plus 1 teaspoon flour

1/4 teaspoon baking soda

1/2 teaspoon ground cinnamon

1/2 teaspoon ground nutmeg

Chess Pie

This timeless Southern queen bows to no king, and with a gooey mixture of vanilla, sugar, and cornmeal, she's got enough class, and enough sass, to beguile every knight, bishop, rook, and pawn in the kingdom. Checkmate.

FOR THE CRUST

One 9-inch unbaked pastry pie crust

INGREDIENTS

1/2 cup butter, melted

2 cups sugar

1 teaspoon vanilla extract

4 large eggs, lightly beaten

1 tablespoon cornmeal

1/4 cup evaporated milk

1 tablespoon white vinegar

whipped cream (optional)

TO PREPARE

Preheat the oven to 450°F. In a large bowl, mix the butter, sugar, and vanilla together. Mix in the eggs, then stir in the cornmeal, evaporated milk, and vinegar until smooth. Pour into pie crust.

Place pie pan on cookie sheet and put in oven. Immediately turn down to 350°F and bake for 45–50 minutes. The cornmeal causes the top to brown, so make sure it doesn't get too brown, and cover with aluminum foil if necessary. The pie is set when a knife inserted in the center comes out clean. Remove from oven and let cool completely.

FOR THE GARNISH

Serve with whipped cream, if desired.

Old-Fashioned Buttermilk Pie

Originally developed in the UK, this pie has become a mainstay in the American South and has evolved into the Amish farmer's favorite. The slight tang of the buttermilk makes this pie a great anytime snack and goes well with a cup of coffee or a spot of tea.

TO PREPARE

Preheat oven to 400°F. In a large bowl, beat eggs and sugar together. Add flour and mix together. Slowly add buttermilk, butter, and vanilla until thoroughly incorporated. Pour into unbaked pie crust. Dust top with ground nutmeg. Place on a baking sheet and bake at 400°F for 20 minutes. Reduce heat to 350°F and continue baking for 30–40 minutes, or until pie is set.

FOR THE GARNISH

Serve with whipped cream, if desired.

FOR THE CRUST

One 9-inch unbaked pastry pie crust

INGREDIENTS

4 large eggs

3/4 cup sugar

1/4 cup all-purpose flour

1 1/2 cups buttermilk

1/4 cup butter, melted

2 teaspoons vanilla extract

1/8 teaspoon ground nutmeg

whipped cream (optional)

Strawberry Eggnog Pie

A perfect segue from frosty winter into spring, the strawberries brighten an already luscious whirlpool of cream and custard, shaping a treat as comfortable on a picnic blanket as it is next to a warming fire.

FOR THE CRUST

One 9-inch baked pastry pie crust

INGREDIENTS

1 teaspoon unflavored gelatin

2 tablespoons cold water

3/4 cup milk, scalded

2 tablespoons cornstarch

1/2 cup sugar

1/2 teaspoon salt

1/4 cup milk

3 large egg yolks, beaten

1 tablespoon butter

1 cup whipped cream

1 tablespoon vanilla extract

strawberry pie filling (p. 40)

TO PREPARE

Place gelatin in a small bowl and add cold water. Scald the milk over low heat, stirring continuously, until bubbles form around the edges. Set aside. Mix together cornstarch, sugar, and salt; add 1/4 cup unscalded milk to mixture. Let cool. Put scalded milk, beaten egg yolks, butter, gelatin, and cornstarch mixture in a saucepan and cook over low heat until thick. Let cool. Fold in whipped cream and vanilla. Pour into pie crust and let set in refrigerator, at least 4 hours. Then top with prepared strawberry pie filling.

Funny Cake Pie

Up is down with this gooey rich reversal of fortune: bake, sit back, and watch as the top layer sinks down to the bottom and the bottom layer rises up. It's funny because it's true. It's delicious because it's cake.

TO PREPARE BOTTOM LAYER

In a bowl, cream shortening and sugar together. Add egg. In a separate bowl, sift baking powder and flour together. Mix vanilla and milk into the egg mixture. Add flour mixture and milk mixture together, alternating one spoonful at a time, starting and ending with the flour mixture. Set aside.

TO PREPARE TOP LAYER

Preheat oven to 350°F. In a bowl, combine sugar and cocoa. Add hot water and vanilla and stir together.

Pour bottom layer over unbaked pastry crust. Pour top layer batter into pan. Make swirls in batter with butter knife. Bake at 350°F for 40 minutes.

FOR THE CRUST

One 9-inch unbaked pastry pastry pie crust

INGREDIENTS
BOTTOM LAYER

1/4 cup shortening

1/2 cup sugar

1 large egg

1 teaspoon baking powder

1 cup all-purpose flour

1/2 teaspoon vanilla extract

1/4 cup whole milk

TOP LAYER

1 cup sugar

1/2 cup cocoa powder

2/3 cup hot water

1/2 teaspoon vanilla extract

Montgomery Pie

Its reputation may be understated, but the taste of this unpretentious Pennsylvania Dutch pie is anything but. Made with lemon and molasses, it's big on flavor, yet simple to make.

FOR THE CRUST

One 9-inch unbaked pastry pie crust

FOR THE FILLING

1/2 cup dark molasses

1/2 cup superfine sugar

3 large eggs, divided

1 cup water

2 tablespoons all-purpose flour

3 tablespoons fresh lemon juice

1 tablespoon lemon zest

1/4 cup butter, softened

2/3 cup sugar

1 1/4 cups all-purpose flour

1/2 teaspoon baking soda

1/2 cup buttermilk

Preheat the oven to 375°F. In a bowl, combine the molasses, sugar, 2 eggs, water, flour, lemon juice, and zest. Mix thoroughly and pour into unbaked pie crust. In another bowl, cream butter with remaining sugar; add 1 egg and beat thoroughly. In another bowl, sift the remaining flour and baking soda together. Add to the creamed mixture, alternating with the buttermilk. Spread over top mixture in pie crust. Bake 35–40 minutes.

Green Tomato Pie

Eating your greens has never tasted so good. Baked inside a tender, flaky crust, this deep South favorite is a delight throughout the summer season.

TO PREPARE

Preheat oven to 425°F. Place tomato slices on paper towels. In a large bowl, mix together the flour, salt, cinnamon, and sugar. Add tomatoes, lemon juice, and vinegar. Spoon mixture into pie crust. Dot with butter and cover with top crust. Bake at 425°F for 10 minutes. Reduce temperature to 350°F and continue baking for 30 minutes.

FOR THE CRUST

One 9-inch unbaked pastry pie crust

INGREDIENTS

3 cups green tomatoes, thinly sliced

3 tablespoons flour

1 teaspoon salt

1 teaspoon ground cinnamon

1 1/4 cup sugar

3 tablespoons lemon juice

1 tablespoon white vinegar

1 tablespoon butter

Funeral Pie

Because of its simplicity, this pie is commonly served at the wake preceding a funeral. The filling is made up of pantry staples, so it can be made at a moment's notice whenever the need arises.

FOR THE CRUST

Two 9-inch unbaked pastry pie crusts

INGREDIENTS

1 cup raisins

2 cups water

1 1/2 cups sugar

4 tablespoons all-purpose flour

1 large egg, well beaten

juice of one lemon

2 teaspoons grated lemon peel

dash salt

FOR THE FILLING

In a large bowl, add raisins to hot water and let soak for 3 hours. In a separate bowl, mix sugar, flour, and egg together. Then add add lemon juice, lemon peel, salt, and egg mixture to the raisins. Place mixture into a saucepan and cook together for 15 minutes over medium heat, stirring occasionally until mixture is thick and bubbly. Once the mixture has thickened, remove from heat and let cool. When the mixture is cool, empty into a a pie-dough lined pie plate. Cover pie with a lattice crust and bake at 400°F for 25 minutes or until browned.

A Slice of Amish Life: Lancaster, PA

Although I have a PhD in pie eating, I knew before writing a pie cookbook that I'd have to go back to school, and pie Harvard is located in Lancaster, Pennsylvania. Lancaster is a different world from my own, a full-time Amish and Mennonite community with deep roots, historical significance, and a diverse population of Plain folk.

Now, I love Pinecraft, my tiny little outpost in the heart of coastal Sarasota, but we're a vacation spot, a place to kick back and relax. There's no clip-clopping of horse hooves—there's shuffleboard and ice cream. Our strength comes from the stories we share and create together.

But Lancaster County shoulders the heritage of Pennsylvania Dutch culture. Its people know that, and they honor it. They work hard. It's not a vacation spot. Those Lancaster women are busy, busy little bees.

Because of these unique differences, I traveled there a ways back with a friend of mine, our aim to find Amish bakers and learn their secrets. We flew up on a warm autumn afternoon, my friend and I comparing strategies like Sherlock Holmes and Watson. We were detectives and our quarry Amish pies—cream, fruit, or savory: those mischievous taste bandits stealing hearts and growing waistlines from Bangor, Maine, to the Tijuana border.

Some of the greatest bakers in the world live in Lancaster. If everyday supermarket ingredients are the stone, and delicious pie is gold, then the bakers up north are the alchemists; they weave hypnotic threads of custard, crumb, cake, and confection into a new vision, a new element of sumptuous force.

To give Thoreau an edible adaptation: these are the pies that try men's souls.

I brought enough plain dresses to last me a week: light blue, pink, dark blue, dark purple, orange, and yellow, and we checked into a quaint little bed-and-breakfast nook near the unfortunately named town of Intercourse, where thousands of tourists flock each year.

Intercourse, Bird-In-Hand, Ronks, Lititz, and other small towns in Lancaster County cluster along fifteen miles of Highway 340, or Old Philadelphia Pike, in central Pennsylvania, forming an "Amish Main Street" of sorts for tourists seeking quasi-authentic buggy rides, sturdy furniture, and gospel-inspired dinner theatre.

Highway 340 was my point of departure, and apparently our arrival was expected; on our first morning, I woke to find a delightful handwritten invitation to a pie party slipped underneath the front door of our B&B. The invitation was on nice card stock and was addressed to "Sherry Gore, Editor of one of Lancaster's favorite magazines, *Cooking & Such*." It was enough for me to get a little weepy over my morning tea. I quickly responded yes.

What I didn't know at the time, however, was that this trip would be an apex, a place where I'd take my feelings for pie to dangerous heights. It was here I flew too close to the sun and almost fell into the sea, like Icarus.

Only I was drowning in custard.

The pie party wasn't for a few days, so my travel companion and I aimed for the boutique shops dimpling the lush green farmlands giving Lancaster its reputation as a homespun paradise.

The Tomato Pie Café was first on our journey, and I have to admit that

I didn't know tomato pies existed. Already I was learning! The Café, billed as "A Little Food. A Little Coffee. A Lot of Charm!" featured a cool urban diner motif, checkered beige floors, and cherry paneling nestled into tiny Lititz, Pennsylvania. This family-owned bistro charmed us the minute we saw its green stilted colonial archways out front.

I ordered the tomato pie (of course), and I had to control my emotions when a savory tomato pie with a cracker crust, topped with mozzarella, jack, and Parmesan cheeses, plopped down in front of me. A clue, Dr. Watson!

The pie wasn't sour or sweet. It was bold, it was cheesy, and it was stuffed with basil and garlic. There was a dash of butter and a mayonnaise twist. The pie pastry crust was rich and full, and toward the end of my slice the crust had sopped up so much of the creamy filling I wasn't sure who had eaten more tomatoes—me or the crust.

So of course, in order to make sure I got my money's worth, I ate that crust too.

The taste was so intriguing that I asked to meet the owners, the Fisher family. They loved my stories of Sarasota, and coincidently enough had considered opening a store down there for some time.

"Please do!" I told them. Sarasota could use whatever the Fishers were offering. I had no idea, until the they introduced me to the tomato pie, that you could fold up the best day of summer and stuff it inside of a pie crust.

And that's exactly how their pie tasted.

Later that day, while visiting the Green Dragon Farmer's Market and Auction, I ate fried pies just like the ones I used to make while living in a Burkesville, Kentucky, Amish community years ago. My daughter Shannon and I would sell one hundred fried pies every Friday, and for a time it was the only income for our family of four.

To make a fried pie, we'd make a crust and then cut a six-inch circle out of the middle, where we'd pour our pie filling. Then we'd fold the crust over top of the filling, pinch the edges, and deep-fry the whole thing. Those pies we made were absolutely delicious and offensively decadent, kind of like deep-frying a Snickers bar: you know it's not good for you, but you don't care once you're eating it. And the fried pies at the Green Dragon were every bit as tasty as the ones I labored over so many years ago.

We also traveled to Zern's Farmer's Market, just a hair's drive from Lancaster County, so that I could visit an Amish-owned pie shop. The store was unique in that the owner sat on a stool in the middle of a circular glass counter filled with pies of all sorts. He seemed to be on a throne, the "Lord of the Pies," and whenever a customer made an order, he'd reach underneath the counter to get their pie, then immediately replace that pie with an identical one in the glass counter.

Never did a pie get purchased and not get immediately replaced. There was always another pie. It was strange. He would reach down every time and come back up with a pie. I imagined there was a hinged door underneath, where a pie magically appeared whenever he wished. *Maybe this is the eternal spring,* I wondered, *where all pies originate.* Maybe it was the first cause. The primordial pie.

It was, for lack of a better phrase, a never-ending fountain of tooth!

And what pies did they have? Blackberry, black raspberry, cherry, ground cherry, sour cherry, apple, red raspberry, pecan, rhubarb, peach, concord grape, etc.

All of the pies were fruit or nut pies, because, as an Old Order Amish business, they couldn't own the refrigeration system needed to keep cream pies cool.

I asked the owner how long his pies would stay fresh sitting out on the counter and, with a slight smile, he answered:

"Nobody knows. One's never lasted long enough to find out."

I guess it's another one of those unanswerable questions, like how many licks it takes to get to the center of a Tootsie Roll Pop: nobody knows.

How long will an Amish fruit pie stay fresh on a counter? Nobody knows.

Grape Pie. That was the handmade sign at the side of the road. We were on the road. I saw the sign.

You can guess what we did.

The roadside stand was tended by an Old Order Mennonite man who'd lived most of his life within three miles of where we stood. He already had his pumpkins out for the fall because it comes early in Lancaster. His wife worked out in the field behind the stand, in a small prairie flower print dress and the same black lace-up boots like my daughter Jacinda used to wear when we lived in Kentucky.

The man was gracious and quiet, happy to have us stop but not overly excited to share more information than was needed.

"Is this your stand?" I asked.

"Yep," he said.

"Do you make all the pies?"

"Yep," he said.

"Do you grow your own grapes?"

"Yep," he said.

I almost wanted to ask him, "Can I have one for free?" just to make sure he could say something else, but I wasn't sure how he'd take a joke. So I settled for gazing at the grape pie.

It was purple, and I don't mean violet. I mean candy-colored kids' school crayons purple. The grapes looked so rich through the lattice crust overtop that, as I bit into a slice, I expected a sophisticated taste, like a sour grape juice.

But I was so wrong. Without thinking, I reached for some Wonderbread and a scoop of peanut butter: the pie tasted just like grape jelly!

As I said, it was no dark violet. It was purple. Just like a kid's crayon and just as fun.

For three days in Lancaster County, I was still an observer, a taster, still on the outside; but I wanted to be on the inside—in the kitchens where these pies were thought up, baked, and perfected.

I eventually found my way into Amish homes by the simplest of measures: I just went up and asked. Many people were delighted by my own personal story and my work with *Cooking & Such* magazine. Some also recognized me from articles I've written for *The Budget*—the 120 year-old Amish newspaper.

My most successful visit to an Amish home was when I met Lydia, a woman who has subscribed to my magazine since the beginning. She invited me into her kitchen to make a very special pie. Lydia was young, maybe twenty-two or so, and had been married the previous summer.

She told me all about her Amish courtship, how her husband had noticed her from afar during a youth volleyball game. She was a Penguin (the Amish churches in Lancaster run large youth groups named after animals; the groups intermingle and play sports, and sometimes even have dances) and he was a Sparrow. It was love at first sight.

As she told me her story of young romance, we made the pie served at her Amish wedding supper. The pie was chocolate mint, and I was *so shocked* (and so tickled) to see her pull an electric-powered Kitchenaid mixer from a secret compartment underneath her kitchen counter! The mixer was mounted to a board on a hinge that swiveled out from a dark cabinet, and I had to suppress my giggles as she powered it on without a hint of shame. It was the only piece of electricity in the whole house—they even had battery-operated lights in the bathroom. But for pie? No expense was spared and no rule couldn't be bent.

Lydia had found love as a Penguin, and I found love after biting into the pie she made. It had a chocolate cookie crust with filling made from homemade marshmallow cream, and chocolate mint pieces crumbled on top.

She went into another room to get her diary, and she read some of the most lovely passages I've ever heard—passages about her husband's kindness, her fear of letting herself become vulnerable to someone else. She wrote of her excitement when he asked her to be his wife, her hopes for their home together, her dreams of a family. Through all of this, so deeply moving, I couldn't get that pie out of my head. How could something taste so deep, like a well?

It was because she'd baked her own self into that pie, her heart and her dreams. Her dreams had come true, and the pie testified. It testified that good things happen to good people.

And that always tastes just right.

On my last day in Lancaster County, I attended the pie party. It must have been the happiest group of ladies I've ever met. The party was at the home of a small and meek Mennonite woman. She had transformed her house into a festive pie banquet hall, replete with colorful table coverings, delicate china dishes, bows, balloons, ribbon, one large table smothered in savory pie dishes, and another drowning in crème.

She was so excited to have us that she began spooning pie into my mouth before both feet hit the rug; I think I had two pieces of the onion pie before I'd greeted all of the invitees.

Let's stop a second and discuss onion pie. I know the party is important for the story, but onion pie is important to my life. And this is my book, which means I get to stop sometimes and smell the roses.

I fell in love with that onion pie at first taste. It was an emotional connection. The filling was based in a beef broth, and it was served in a buttery pastry-cream cracker crust with cheese on top. It tasted like French onion soup—but only the top, most delicious, cheesy part we all secretly buy the soup for. I felt richer having had that pie, like when someone makes a friend so dear it's impossible to imagine life before they were around: "Who did I call back then? What did I do?"

Only, that friend was onion pie. And I couldn't believe we hadn't met before.

Of course, I had to eventually move on, and I tasted every pie at least once. It was my second run-in with a tomato pie, and I learned that what I'd tasted at the Tomato Pie Café wasn't exactly a trade secret—these pies were delicious everywhere.

We all took turns sampling the dishes; there were a lot of "oohs and aahs" (many, to be frank, coming from yours truly), and I laughed to myself upon realizing I could tell who baked each pie by whose back straightened with pride as an "ooh" or an "aah" sounded out; sometimes so many people were enjoying so many pies at once that the women straightening with pride popped up and down like a whack-a-mole carnival game.

The people were all so nice to me, and they were all so fascinated that I was so fascinated with pie. And after we'd tasted all the pies, we had whoopie pies. For dessert!

It was quickly necessary then for the whole bunch of us to take off on a walk to burn up some calories. We were close to downtown Lititz, and so we made a nice afternoon stroll through that beautiful red brick and sleepy hamlet.

But no sooner had we burned enough calories to fill half a pie crust than we found ourselves standing under the iconic Wilbur Chocolates Co. white-and-brown hand-painted sign, which announces the spot of some of the best chocolate on earth.

So of course we sat down and ate some delicious chocolate. And I took the opportunity to score a good tip about making perfect desserts from Wilbur's head chocolatier: add more sugar.

Our few days in Lancaster passed more quickly than I expected, and though I was loath to leave such beautiful land, people, and pie behind, I was ready to make the trip back home and apply what I'd learned to my own kitchen. I felt like I'd been to a holy land, and now felt the responsibility of an evangelical. I would convert the masses; I would open their eyes to the full truth of the Pie.

As an aside (because I can do that), I will say that our trip home was uneventful, other than that I boarded our flight home seven pounds heavier than when I'd left.

And it wasn't in the luggage.

I'd spent almost eight full days thinking, talking, and eating pie, and I must admit that it was heaven. I was enthralled. We were perfect together, me and pie. Lockstep. Nothing could stand between us, I thought.

But dark clouds were on the horizon. Perfection doesn't last. And I would find out soon enough that too much of a good thing isn't a great thing. Sometimes a spoonful of sugar doesn't help the medicine go down very well at all.

Chapter Seven

Cutie Pies

These are the "Shirley Temples" of the pie world: a charming assortment of sprite-sized desserts nimble enough to dance over your taste buds, and brimming with enough talent to light up the sky. Perfect for a starring role at birthday parties, elegant weddings, baby showers, potlucks, and warm Sunday afternoons, these cuties sparkle next to any dish and raise any spread to the level of true art. These entertaining pies may be petite, but there is nothing miniature about their taste.

Fried Pies

An essential goody at Amish bake sales, fried pies are a wonderful treat. Cherries, peaches, blackberry, even coconut cream—any fruit or pudding filling will work. So use your imagination and start frying!

TO PREPARE

In a bowl, soak apple chunks in water. In small saucepan, cook apples and water over medium heat until the apples are tender. Remove from heat and drain off the juice. Place apples into a large bowl. Add sugar, butter, cinnamon, and nutmeg to apples. Keep mixture refrigerated until ready to assemble.

TO ASSEMBLE

Roll out dough to 1/8-inch thickness and cut in 6-inch circles. Place 2 heaping tablespoons filling on one side. Fold dough to make a half-moon shape. Crimp edges with bit of water to completely seal.

TO FRY

Deep fry the pies in vegetable oil (heated to about 350°F) for about 4 minutes or until golden brown. Drain on paper towels. Let cool completely before eating.

FOR THE GARNISH

If desired, make a sugar glaze using 1 pound of confectioners' sugar, 1 teaspoon vanilla, and 1 tablespoon corn syrup. Add water, 1 teaspoon at a time, until desired consistency is reached. Dip hot pies into glaze and place on cooking racks to cool.

FOR THE CRUST

One double recipe for pastry pie crust

INGREDIENTS

2 cups dried apples, chunked

1 1/3 cups water

1/2 cup sugar

2 heaping tablespoons butter

1 teaspoon ground cinnamon

1/8 teaspoon ground nutmeg

FOR THE SUGAR GLAZE

1 pound confectioners' sugar

1 teaspoon vanilla

1 tablespoon corn syrup

Pies in a Jar

Tie those apron strings and turn any cooking station into a farmhouse kitchen. It's easy to make your favorite pies in these miniature canning jars. They are as delicious as they are adorable—perfect for parties and picnics!

FOR THE CRUST

One double recipe pastry pie crust

1/2 pint wide-mouth canning jars

FOR THE FILLING

One recipe using your favorite fruit filling (if using apple, chop apples into small pieces)

sanding sugar, optional

TO PREPARE

Wash and dry jars before using. Roll out pie dough slightly thinner than you would for a regular pie. Cut into pieces and press into jars three-fourths of the way up the sides of the jar. Spoon in pie filling until the jar is three-fourths full. Use a canning jar lid as a template for the diameter of the top crust. Make decorative cut-outs using tiny cookie cutters, if desired. Place the dough circles over jars, gently pressing dough in the center and on the sides. Add cut-out dough pieces. Sprinkle with sanding sugar if desired. Pies may be frozen with lids on for later use.

FOR FRESH BAKING

Place jars on baking sheet and bake at 375°F for 45 minutes. Cover jars loosely with aluminum foil if the tops brown too quickly. You want to be sure the bottom crust bakes thoroughly. Allow jars to cool to the touch before serving.

TO BAKE FROM FROZEN

Place frozen jars on baking sheet. Remove lids. Bake at 350°F for 1 hour. Allow jars to cool to the touch before serving.

Makes about 12 pie jars, depending on thickness of crust.

Blueberry Turnovers

Mmm! Make these tasty fruit turnovers for a nostalgic treat that is sure to take center stage wherever they appear. Be prepared to double the recipe for seconds. These boisterous, tart, juicy pies summon standing ovations from audiences everywhere. Bravo!

FOR THE FILLING

In a saucepan, gently cook blueberries in 1 cup of water over low heat for a few minutes. Mix sugar, cornstarch, and salt together in a bowl, add to blueberry mixture, and cook until thick. Add lemon juice, vanilla, and almond extract. Let cool.

TO ASSEMBLE

Roll pastry out to an even thickness and cut out 8-inch circles. Place several tablespoons of pie filling on one side of each turnover. Fold over and pinch edges closed. Crimp with fork. Place pies on a parchment-paper lined baking sheet. Sprinkle each turnover with sanding sugar. Bake at 450°F for 10 minutes. Turn temperature down to 350°F and continue baking for 35–40 minutes, until golden brown.

TIP: You may substitute your favorite fruit pie filling for the center.

FOR THE CRUST

One double recipe pastry pie crust

INGREDIENTS

2 cups fresh or frozen blueberries

1 cup water

3 tablespoons sugar

1 tablespoon plus 1 teaspoon cornstarch

1/8 teaspoon salt

1 tablespoon lemon juice

1/4 teaspoon vanilla extract

1/8 teaspoon almond extract

sanding sugar

Pie Pops

Let your imagination run wild with this recipe. You can use cookie cutters to create unique shapes, or go for a more rustic look. Tied with a fancy ribbon, these make cute party favors.

WHAT YOU'LL NEED

pastry pie dough

cookie cutters

lollipop sticks (can be purchased in any craft department)

your favorite fruit pie filling

egg wash

parchment paper

ribbon

TO PREPARE

Preheat oven to 375°F. Roll pastry dough on floured surface and cut desired shapes with 3-inch cookie cutter. Use a tiny cutter to make decorative design, if desired. Place bottom pastry piece on parchment-lined baking sheet. Center lollipop stick onto bottom of dough. Add 1 full teaspoon pie filling. Cover with top pastry and crimp edges. Place decorative cut-out piece of pastry (if desired) on top of pie pop. Brush tops of pastry with egg wash. Bake at 375°F for 15 minutes. Let cool completely before removing from pan. Tie with ribbon and share!

FOR CHERRY CHOCOLATE PIE POPS

Use 4 chocolate chips and 1 teaspoon cherry pie filling for each pie pop.

Makes about 3 dozen pie pops.

Pie Parfaits

In a conundrum over what to do with a crust that turns out looking less than stellar? Turn your faux pas into fabulous by serving your pie in pretty parfait glasses.

TO ASSEMBLE

Crumble pie crust and layer a couple of tablespoons in each glass. Spoon in the pie filling, then add the whipped cream. Repeat layers up the glass until you reach the top. These parfaits make a beautiful presentation. They're also something to make in a pinch for company if you're not happy with how your baked pie crust turned out.

WHAT YOU'LL NEED

6 tall parfait glasses

6 long spoons

One 9-inch baked pastry, cookie, shortbread, graham cracker, or gingerbread crust

1 recipe your favorite fruit, cream, or pudding pie filling

whipped cream

Pie Straws

Turn those extra pie crust bits into a whimsical treat your little ones can snack on while your masterpiece is baking.

INGREDIENTS

Scraps of pastry dough

melted butter

1/4 cup sugar

2 teaspoons ground cinnamon

TO PREPARE

Preheat oven to 375°F. Cut pie crust scraps into strips with a fluted pastry wheel. Brush strips with melted butter. In a small bowl, mix together sugar and cinnamon. Sprinkle strips with a cinnamon sugar mixture. Bake at 375°F for 15 minutes. Once cool, these make a tasty treat dipped in jam.

Chocolate Whoopie Pies

These little cream-filled cakes may have originated in Maine, but Pennsylvania made them popular. It's said this treat earned its amusing name when Amish boys and girls were so delighted to discover one in their lunch box they shouted, "Whoopie!"

TO PREPARE

Preheat oven to 350°F. Line baking sheets with parchment paper.

Cream together the lard and sugar in a bowl. Add eggs and vanilla. In another large bowl, sift together flour, cocoa, and salt. Add to lard and sugar mixture alternately with buttermilk. Dissolve baking soda in hot water; add to mixture. Beat well. Drop heaping tablespoons of the dough onto the prepared baking sheets, about 3 inches apart. Bake for 10 to 12 minutes, until the tops feel firm and a toothpick inserted into the center of the cookie comes out clean. Remove from oven and let cool on baking sheets for 10 minutes before removing to a wire rack to cool completely.

Cream shortening and milk in a large bowl. Add confectioners' sugar and vanilla; mix well. Beat in egg whites until filling is fluffy.

Turn half of the cooled cookies upside down, flat side facing up, and spread with filling. Place another cookie, flat side down, on top of the filling. Repeat until all cookies are used.

INGREDIENTS

1 ½ cups lard or shortening

3 cups sugar

3 large eggs, beaten

3 teaspoons vanilla extract

6 cups all-purpose flour

1 ½ cups cocoa powder

3 teaspoons salt

1 ½ cups buttermilk or sour milk

3 teaspoons baking soda

1 ½ cups hot water

CREAM FILLING

1 ½ cups white shortening (do not use butter flavored)

5 tablespoons milk

3 cups confectioners' sugar

1 tablespoon vanilla extract

3 large egg whites, beaten stiff

Lemon Whoopie Pies

The refreshingly cool taste of this treat is an upscale version of its chocolate counterpart with its delicate cream cheese filling.

INGREDIENTS

1 1/2 cups all-purpose flour

1/2 teaspoon baking powder

1/4 teaspoon baking soda

1/4 teaspoon salt

6 tablespoons butter, room temperature

1 cup sugar

1 teaspoon lemon zest

1 large egg

1 tablespoon lemon juice

1 teaspoon vanilla extract

1/2 cup buttermilk

LEMON CREAM CHEESE FILLING

6 tablespoons butter, softened

6 ounces cream cheese, softened

1 teaspoon vanilla extract

1 teaspoon lemon zest

2 tablespoons lemon juice

2 3/4 cups confectioners' sugar

Preheat oven to 350°. Line 2 baking sheets with parchment paper.

In a medium bowl, sift together the flour, baking powder, baking soda, and salt.

In the bowl of an electric stand mixer fitted with the paddle attachment, beat the butter, sugar, and lemon zest on medium speed until smooth, about 3 minutes. Add the egg, lemon juice, and vanilla, mixing until blended, about 1 minute. Reduce the mixer speed to low and add half of the flour mixture, mixing until just combined. Mix in the buttermilk. Mix in the remaining flour mixture until just combined.

Drop heaping tablespoons of the dough onto the prepared baking sheets, about 3 inches apart. Bake for 10–12 minutes, until the tops feel firm and a toothpick inserted into the center of the cookie comes out clean. Remove from oven and let cool on baking sheets for 10 minutes before removing to a wire rack to cool completely.

Once cool, make the filling. In a bowl, beat the butter, cream cheese, vanilla, lemon zest, and lemon juice until thoroughly blended and smooth. Add the confectioners' sugar and mix until smooth.

Turn half of the cooled cookies upside down, flat side up, and spread with filling. Place another cookie, flat side down, on top of the filling. Repeat until all cookies are used. These little pies are great when chilled.

Chapter Eight

Savory Pies and Quiches

When people think of pie, they think of dessert—
and who could blame them—but the savvy baker never forgets
the savory pie, that warm and hearty makeshift masterpiece, that
gruff answer to a raging appetite, when it's time to batten down the
hatches and get down to the nourishing nitty gritty. Real men *do*
eat quiche after all, at least they do when it's emblazoned with thick
sausage and spicy roasted red peppers. And they'll take their share
of plump pot pies, chummy clam chowder, heavenly deep-dish
French onion, farmhouse chicken, and hearty beef stew too. The
savory pies own dinner, and it's always a shame when they're cleared
away for dessert but, to be honest, I've never been one to argue.

Summer Tomato Pie

This savory pie is a tasty way to use up ripe tomatoes from the garden. The sophisticated taste of a cheesy crust combined with the flavor of fresh basil make a delectable summertime medley for even the most discriminating connoisseur.

TO PREPARE

Preheat oven to 350°F. Bake pie crust for 20 minutes.

Scald, peel, and seed the tomatoes. Then roughly chop the tomatoes. (Tomatoes may be left to drain for 20–30 minutes in a colander.) Use paper towels to remove any excess liquid. Cover the bottom of the baked pie crust with chopped onion. Add chopped tomatoes to cover the onions. Sprinkle the chopped basil over the tomatoes. In a medium bowl, mix together the grated cheese, mayonnaise, and hot sauce. Season with salt and pepper. Cover tomatoes with grated cheese mixture. Place in oven and bake until browned, about 25–45 minutes.

FOR THE CRUST

One 9-inch unbaked pastry pie crust

INGREDIENTS

4 fresh tomatoes

1/4 yellow or white onion, chopped

1/4 cup fresh basil, chopped

2 cups grated cheese (combination of sharp Cheddar, Monterey Jack, and Swiss)

3/4 cup mayonnaise

1 teaspoon of bottled cayenne pepper sauce

salt and black pepper to taste

Farmhouse Chicken Pot Pie

Chicken pot pie is the ultimate comfort food. This recipe is great anytime of the year. Dress it up for special occasions by adding mushrooms and baking in individual ramekins.

FOR THE CRUST

Two 9-inch unbaked pastry pie crusts

INGREDIENTS

1/3 cup butter

1/3 cup all-purpose flour

1/3 cup chopped onion

1/2 teaspoon salt

1/4 – 1/2 teaspoon black pepper

1 3/4 cups chicken broth

2/3 cup heavy cream

2 cups cooked chicken, diced

2 potatoes, peeled, boiled, and cubed

1 1/2 cups fresh vegetables, cooked until tender-firm or 1 (10-ounce) package frozen mixed vegetables

egg wash

TO PREPARE

Preheat oven to 425°F. Melt butter in saucepan. Blend in flour, onion, salt, and pepper. Cook over low heat, stirring constantly, until smooth and bubbly. Remove from heat. Stir in the broth and cream. Return to heat and bring to a boil over medium heat, stirring constantly. Boil and stir 1 minute. Add chicken, potatoes, and vegetables and remove from heat. Set aside. Line pie plate with prepared bottom crust. Pour in filling. Top with top crust. Score top in center to vent. Flute edges as desired. Brush crust with egg wash. Cook uncovered in 425°F oven 30–35 minutes, or until golden brown.

Thanksgiving Pie

The Pilgrims could only dream of these sorts of fixin's during the first Thanksgiving, and it's a good thing too: they might've spent all their time with this inventive pie, made up of Thanksgiving leftovers, and forgotten about that "discovering a new land" idea altogether.

TO PREPARE

Preheat oven to 350°F. Line a pie plate with an unbaked crust. Place turkey in the bottom of the crust. Cover with mashed potatoes. Pour 1 cup of gravy over the turkey. Add a layer of cranberry sauce. Spoon stuffing over the cranberry sauce. Pour on remaining gravy. Sprinkle with pepper. Cover with top crust and flute edges.

Use a cream or egg wash and score top crust. Place pie plate on baking sheet. Bake for 45 minutes or until golden brown.

FOR THE CRUST

Two 9-inch unbaked pastry pie crusts

INGREDIENTS

12 ounces thick-sliced boneless turkey breast

2 cups buttered mashed potatoes

2 cups turkey gravy, divided

1 ounce dried cranberries or $1/2$ cup cranberry sauce

2 cups prepared herb seasoned stuffing

$1/4$ teaspoon cracked black pepper

cream or egg wash

Hearty Beef Pot Pie

Steer the man in your life to the dinner table with this hearty and robust pie, a rugged belly filler slathered in rich gravy and covered with a blanket of golden brown flaky crust.

FOR THE CRUST

Two 9-inch unbaked pastry pie crusts

INGREDIENTS

1 pound beef stew meat, cut in 1-inch cubes

1 cup milk

1 1/3 cups flour, divided

6 tablespoons butter

1 tablespoon oil

1 small onion, diced

2 cups beef broth, divided

1 teaspoon minced garlic

salt and black pepper to taste

1 1/2 cups potatoes, peeled, cubed, and cooked

1 cup frozen peas and carrots

1 stalk celery, diced

TO PREPARE

Preheat oven to 450°F. Place meat in a bowl and soak in 1 cup of milk for 5 minutes, then drain meat and dredge in 1 cup of flour. Shake off excess. Place meat in a skillet and brown in butter and oil on all sides over medium high heat. Add onion before meat is completely browned. Turn down heat to low. Add 1 cup broth and garlic, salt, and pepper and let simmer for 20 minutes. In a bowl, whisk 1/3 cup flour into 1 cup broth. Add to pan. Add the potatoes, peas and carrots, and celery to the pan and continue cooking until the beef is tender and the mixture is thick and bubbly. Pour the mixture into an unbaked pie crust. Top with crust. Score the top crust to vent. Bake at 450°F for 35 minutes, or until crust is golden brown.

Deep-Dish French Onion Pie

Ooh la la! This unusual pie tastes like the classic French soup. It is a wonderfully filling lunch or dinner treat. Délicieux!

TO PREPARE

In a bowl, combine butter and cracker crumbs together and press into the bottom and sides of a 9-inch pie plate.

Preheat oven to 350°F. In a large skillet, lightly sauté onion slices over medium heat in butter to soften and bring out the sweet flavor. Remove the onions from pan and set aside. In a bowl, combine eggs, milk, beef stock, garlic, thyme, salt, and pepper. Place sautéed onions in pie plate. Pour egg mixture over the top. Sprinkle with shredded cheese. Cover the pan loosely with aluminum foil. Bake for 20 minutes. Remove foil and continue baking for an additional 15 minutes. The top should be a beautiful, light golden brown. Let set for 5 minutes before serving.

FOR THE CRUST

1/4 cup butter, melted

1 1/2 cups (about one sleeve) saltine crackers, finely crushed

INGREDIENTS

2 yellow onions, thinly sliced and halved

2 tablespoons butter

3 large eggs, beaten

1/4 cup evaporated milk or cream

1/3 cup seasoned beef stock

1 clove garlic, minced

1/4 teaspoon dried thyme

1/4 teaspoon salt

1/4 teaspoon cracked black pepper

1 cup Gruyere or Swiss cheese, shredded

Seafood Chowder Pot Pie

The succulent ingredients in this catch of the day are tenderly tucked inside a flaky crust to pack a wallop that will reel you in on waves of maritime delight. Don't let this be the "one that got away."

FOR THE CRUST

Two 9-inch unbaked pastry pie crusts. For an extravagant pie, use garlic and Cheddar pastry crust

INGREDIENTS

1 1/2 cups diced potatoes

1 cup carrots, chopped

1/2 cup celery, chopped

1/2 cup onion, diced

1/2 pound crab meat

1/2 pound shrimp, peeled and cooked

2 teaspoons chicken base

6 tablespoons butter

4 tablespoons all-purpose flour

2 tablespoons cornstarch

1 cup half-and-half

1 cup milk

1/2 teaspoon salt (or more to taste)

1/2 teaspoon black pepper

1 teaspoon or more Old Bay Seasoning

TO PREPARE

Preheat oven to 425°F. Using a medium stockpot, cook potatoes, carrots, celery, and onion in 4 cups water until soft.

Add the crab, shrimp, and chicken base. In a separate pan, melt butter. Stir in flour, cornstarch, half-and-half, milk, salt, pepper, and Old Bay. Cook on medium to medium-low heat until thickened, stirring often. Add the flour mixture to the vegetable mixture. Pour into the pie crust. Cover with the top crust and seal the edges. Make several small vents in the top crust to allow steam to escape. Bake at 425°F for 30–35 minutes, until the crust is golden brown and the filling is bubbly.

Sausage and Roasted Red Pepper Quiche

The combination of Cheddar cheese and sausage makes this dish the sharpest quiche on the block.

TO PREPARE

Preheat oven to 375°F. In a bowl, whisk evaporated milk and eggs together. Add sausage, salt, pepper, red pepper flakes, and cheeses. Stir in roasted red pepper. Pour into prebaked pie crust. Bake for 20 minutes. Turn down oven temperature to 350°F and continue baking for 15 minutes, or until center is set. Remove from oven and let set 5 minutes before serving.

FOR THE CRUST

One 10-inch deep-dish pastry pie crust, baked for 7–8 minutes

INGREDIENTS

1 cup evaporated milk

6 large eggs, beaten

1 pound sausage, cooked and crumbled

1/4 teaspoon salt

1/2 teaspoon black pepper

dash of red pepper flakes

1/3 cup Parmesan cheese, grated

1 1/2 cups white or yellow cheddar cheese, shredded

3/4 cup roasted red pepper, sliced and drained

Spinach Bacon Cheese Quiche

This light but tasty quiche works well for brunch or a light supper. You had me at bacon.

FOR THE CRUST

One 10-inch deep-dish pastry pie crust

INGREDIENTS

1 pound fresh spinach leaves or 1 (10-ounce) box frozen spinach

3 large eggs, beaten

1/2 cup Parmesan cheese

1 cup Swiss cheese

1 1/2 cups heavy cream

10 slices bacon, cooked and crumbled

1/2 teaspoon salt

1/4 teaspoon black pepper

4 ounces cream cheese, cut into tiny pieces

TO PREPARE

Preheat oven to 350°F. If using frozen spinach, let thaw and squeeze out as much water as possible. For fresh greens, sauté in a pan with a couple tablespoons of water for 5 minutes. Remove from heat and drain.

In a bowl, combine eggs, Parmesan and Swiss cheeses, cream, spinach, bacon, and bacon, salt, and pepper. Fold in cream cheese. Pour into pie crust. Bake for 40 minutes. Let set on counter for 30 minutes before serving.

Million-Dollar Crab Quiche

The ultimate in surf-side cuisine, enjoy this rich quiche without emptying your pockets.

TO PREPARE

Preheat oven to 350°F. Gently fold all ingredients together in a large bowl. Using a rubber spatula, place the mixture into pastry crust. Bake for 35 minutes. The top should be golden brown. Remove from oven and let rest for 10 minutes before serving.

FOR THE CRUST

One 9-inch unbaked pastry pie crust

INGREDIENTS

1 1/2 cups lump crab meat

6 ounces grated Swiss cheese

1 medium potato, cooked, peeled, and cubed

2 scallions, minced

1/4 teaspoon dry mustard

1 tablespoon all-purpose flour

2 large eggs, beaten

1/2 teaspoon salt

1/4 teaspoon black pepper

A Slice of Amish Life: Sarasota, FL

Sometimes in a relationship, a couple can't bear to be apart; a day separated is a day lost forever. It's a wonderfully unique time for those able to hold on to it. But eventually things tend to even out a little, and the need wears off. There's still love, even attraction, but *every day* becomes a little too much. Some people call it settling in, and while it marks the end of one stage, it does set the table for a longer, more stable union.

When I was in Lancaster, I couldn't bear to be separated from those pies. But when I got back to Sarasota and began making them, day after day; tasting them over and over to perfect the ingredients; all in hopes of pre-serving a commitment (to writing a pie book), I finally realized that me, myself, and pie might need to put in a little work to make this thing last.

It all started in the kitchen, as much in my life does. I needed to hone the recipes in this very book because I created a lot of the recipes myself. And I needed to curate and create all of those recipes rather quickly. Deadlines are deadlines, after all.

So I made every pie I could with every recipe I'd cultivated over a life-time. I ate and I ate and I ate—not full pies, of course, just bites of filling or crust—in order to get the ingredients down perfectly; sometimes I had to make a pie eight or nine times before I felt it was ready.

I made so many pies so quickly that I noticed one afternoon a nice sheen to my hair. *Have I switched shampoos?* I asked myself. I checked the bottle in the bathroom; it was the same. *What about conditioner?* I wondered. Nope—it was the same too. But then why did my hair shine so brightly?

"It's probably the shortening, Mom," my son, Tyler, blurted out from the living room where he'd hunkered down to read. "You've got sugar hair."

He was right. I'd been making pie, and on breaks I'd been pulling my hair back or wiping my forehead with the back of my hand. I was literally covered in pie. They say, "You are what you eat," and I guess I was a testament to that at least. I was losing myself. In pie.

In my work, I also needed to experiment in order to find new and exciting tastes. At one point, I made an ultimate pie that I called the "Million-Dollar Crab Quiche," because it includes everything I'd want in a savory pie, and because it doesn't cost a million bucks (but tastes like it should).

I worked on each new recipe one at a time, with a notepad and a pen at my side to record minute changes I'd make in each batch. The kitchen counter would often be covered in used mixing bowls, wooden spoons, overturned pie plates, measuring cups, forks, and ingredient bags. My huge and overstocked blue Hoosier cabinet I'd just leave open, because I never got everything I needed out of it on my first try. Everything was covered in dough. The pages of my notepad stuck together with sugar. My little dog, Winston, was ever-present at my ankles, happy and hopeful that another morsel might fall his way.

The process is messy because I want to get it right. I want the people who've bought this book to be as enamored with these pies as I am. So I don't cut any corners.

When I'm creating a new recipe, I always start with the crust, because I never know beforehand what type of crust will go with the pie I'm envisioning. It could be a pastry or crumb or gingersnap crust, and the crusts themselves need to be tweaked once I taste them along with the filling. So I'll make a couple different crusts while I'm putting together the filling, which I'll then add to each crust and taste. And once I've decided on the crust, the filling has to be tweaked too. This is where my experience as official Pie Contest Judge really comes in handy.

Some of the pies I struggled to perfect were the crab quiche, the tomato pie, the barbeque pulled pork pie, the creamy chicken hand pies, the fudgie go-for-broke brownie pie, the raisin custard, and the caramel. Also the apple skillet pie, which everybody on earth should try at least once.

I also made a difficult-to-get-right-but-delicious-to-eat Thanksgiving pie, with turkey, stuffing, cranberries, homemade whipped mashed potatoes, and butter layered in a pastry pie crust, covered with a double crust over top, and then baked. Oh my, was I giddy when it was in the oven. I couldn't keep away. I'd filled it with all the fixings of a holiday dinner, along with some of the excitement I always feel when fall comes around, because that's when all my Amish and Mennonite friends start showing up in Pinecraft. It was delicious.

But all those pies started taking a toll and, day after day, I raced toward my deadline with determined eyes and sugared hair. As the days turned into weeks, I started to look at all that pie a bit differently. I still loved those pies—every one of them—but I was growing weary. Couldn't

I get a break from time to time? You know, just to be around some other foods? It's important to have hobbies, and it's important to have some independence. Was I too into it all?

Was I feeling smothered? By pie?!

I guess it's possible. I've had so much fun writing the pie book and making the treats inside, but it's been tough on me and pie. We've learned that we're good together, but I think, as I finish off the last few recipes . . . I think pie and I will have to learn to set some limits. We need boundaries. We need some space.

It's not like it's an end. I look at it as a beginning. I love pie, and I hope to have my own pie shop one day. But we need to aim for the long haul. We need time to mature, like the concord grapes in those ridiculous purple pies up in Lancaster County.

We're not a flash in the pan, and so I don't need to treat it as such. I don't want to tax anything. After all, I didn't choose pie—it chose me. And I respect that. So I'll make sure we make it, together.

Me, myself, and pie.

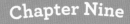

Chapter Nine

Hand Pies

Sometimes all we need in life is a little break in the routine to unlock our best ideas. The crusty hand pie, so named because it fits right in your hand, serves as a juicy answer to baker's block—that moment when you just don't know what to make next. Called "pasties" in England and "empanadas" in Spanish and Latino cultures, hand pies can be filled with the sweet or the savory; salt, sugar, cream, or fruit; and they can be fried or baked, pinched and crimped, folded, squared, rolled, or stuffed into a lucky muffin pan.

But baker beware: these fertile and imaginative treats offer so many delectable designs that you may not ever bake a full-size pie again. So when you reach a fork in the road, and you don't know what to bake next, give it a go with one of these recipes and say good-bye to the ordinary. (And pick up that fork in the road—you'll need it!)

Salted Caramel Apple Hand Pies

This sophisticated little treat will remind you of that quintessential autumn confection, caramel apples, tucked inside of a delicious crust.

FOR THE FILLING:

In a small bowl, combine the apples, lemon juice, cinnamon, sugar, flour, and butter, stirring until thoroughly mixed. Set aside.

TO ASSEMBLE THE PIES:

Preheat the oven to 425°F. Remove the dough from the refrigerator and unfold it onto a well-floured surface, rolling it out to a square or rectangle. Using a circular cookie cutter, cut out an even amount of circles.

Place dough circles on a parchment paper-lined baking sheet. Spoon a small portion of the apple filling into the center of each circle, leaving a border around the filling. Top the apple filling with a portion of the chopped caramels and a pinch of sea salt. Place a second dough circle atop each filled circle, then use a fork to crimp the edges together, sealing each pie. To ensure your pie filling doesn't ooze out and burn, make sure there are no holes in your crust—top or bottom.

Brush each pie with egg or cream wash and, using a sharp knife, cut two or three vents on the top of each pie. Sprinkle the tops with sanding sugar. Bake for 15 minutes, or until golden brown. Let cool.

FOR THE CRUST

One double recipe pastry pie crust

INGREDIENTS

2 cups tart apples, peeled and diced

2 teaspoons lemon juice

1/2 teaspoon ground cinnamon

1/4 cup sugar

2 teaspoons all-purpose flour

2 tablespoons butter

12 soft caramels, chopped fine (homemade caramel recipe on p. 266)

sea salt, flaked or coarse

egg or cream wash

sanding sugar

Barbecue Pulled Pork Hand Pies

These scrumptious pies are perfect for summer picnics and get-togethers. Use your favorite barbecue sauce to customize to your favorite flavors. Try using honey barbecue, smoky, hickory, sweet and tangy, or your own creation. Guaranteed to be lip-smacking good!

FOR THE CRUST

One double recipe unbaked pastry pie crust

INGREDIENTS

2 pounds Boston butt roast

1 can root beer or cola

2 large cloves garlic, minced

1/2 teaspoon salt

1 teaspoon black pepper

Barbecue sauce, about one jar

cream wash

TO PREPARE

Place the pork roast in a slow cooker; pour the soda over the meat. Scatter the top of the roast with the garlic, salt, and pepper. Cover and cook on low until well cooked and the pork shreds easily with a fork. This takes about 6 to 7 hours, depending on your slow cooker. Remove the roast from pan and place in large bowl. Shred the meat with two forks. Add barbecue sauce, thoroughly coating meat.

TO ASSEMBLE

Preheat oven to 425°F. Cut out 8-inch dough circles. Spoon meat mixture into one half of the circle. Fold over and pinch edges closed. Brush on cream wash. Place on a greased cookie sheet. Bake at 425°F for 15 minutes, or until crust is golden brown.

Remove from oven and place on wire cooling rack for 5 minutes. Wrap in parchment paper to serve.

Ham and Cheese Hand Pies

These spicy pies are hearty and filling, perfect for a brunch or afternoon snack. Dill pickle slices make a great addition to these pies when using Cheddar cheese. Cheese: it's good with everything!

TO PREPARE

Preheat oven to 425°F. Combine all of the ingredients together in bowl. Divide the mixture into 6 parts. Roll out the dough and cut out 6 squares. Fill dough on one side of each cut out. Fold over dough, covering mixture, and seal. Crimp edges and seal with water.

FOR THE GARNISH

Place on a greased cookie sheet. Generously brush top of crusts with cream wash. Cut 3 small vents on the top of each pie.

Bake at 425°F for 15 minutes, or until crust is golden brown. Remove from oven and place on wire cooling rack for 5 minutes. Wrap in parchment paper to serve.

FOR THE CRUST

One double recipe pastry pie crust

INGREDIENTS

2 cups Cheddar, pepper jack, Monterey Jack, or Swiss cheese, shredded

2 large eggs, beaten

2 cups ham, cooked and cubed

1 tablespoon butter

2 tablespoons Parmesan cheese (if using Cheddar)

1/4 teaspoon seasoned salt

1/8 teaspoon black pepper

1 jalapeño pepper, seeded and chopped (optional)

cream wash

Jalapeño Popper Hand Pies

This recipe is a fun twist on a popular appetizer and not for the faint of heart. A healthy glass of your favorite cool drink is a recommended standby; though, for some, a fire extinguisher might be a better fit. BANG BANG!

FOR THE CRUST

One double recipe pastry pie crust

FOR THE FILLING

1 (8-ounce) package cream cheese, softened

2 cups shredded cooked chicken

1/3 cup sour cream

4 ounces jalapeño peppers, diced

1/4 teaspoon black pepper

1/2 teaspoon salt

cream wash

TO PREPARE

Preheat oven to 425°F. Combine all of the ingredients together in bowl. Divide the mixture into 6 parts. Roll out the dough and cut out 6 squares. Fill dough on one side of each cut out. Fold over dough, covering mixture, and seal. Crimp edges and seal with water..

Place on a greased cookie sheet. Generously brush top of crusts with cream wash. Cut 3 small vents on the top of each pie

Bake at 425°F for 15 minutes, or until crust is golden brown. Remove from oven and place on wire cooling rack for 5 minutes. Wrap in parchment paper to serve.

Creamy Bacon Chicken Hand Pies

A carefully folded crust corrals a balmy smoky bacon bouquet, which infuses the creamy chicken filling with an arresting pique of breakfast nostalgia. Slice vents into the crust to allow the pie to breathe, and to drive your guests wild with anticipation.

TO PREPARE

Sauté onion and garlic with 2 tablespoon butter in skillet over medium heat until the onion is translucent but not browned. Add cream cheese and mix well.

Add chicken, chopped broccoli, potatoes, and bacon to cream cheese mixture. Stir gently until well combined.

Divide pie dough into 6 pieces. Roll out piece into a rectangle. On one piece of dough, put 1/6 of cream cheese and chicken mixture. Fold dough over the top and pinch seams to seal off. Press edges with fork. Repeat until you have 6 hand pies.

Place on a greased cookie sheet. Generously brush top of crusts with egg wash. Cut 3 small vents on the top of each pie. Bake at 400°F for about 20 minutes, or until tops are golden brown. Remove from oven and place on wire cooling rack for 5 minutes.

Wrap in parchment paper to serve.

FOR THE CRUST

One double recipe pastry pie crust

INGREDIENTS

2 tablespoons onion, minced

1 clove garlic, minced

2 tablespoons butter

6 ounces cream cheese, softened

1 3/4 cups cooked chicken breast, chopped

1 cup cooked broccoli, chopped

1 cup cooked potatoes, cubed

6 slices smoked bacon, cooked and crumbled

egg wash

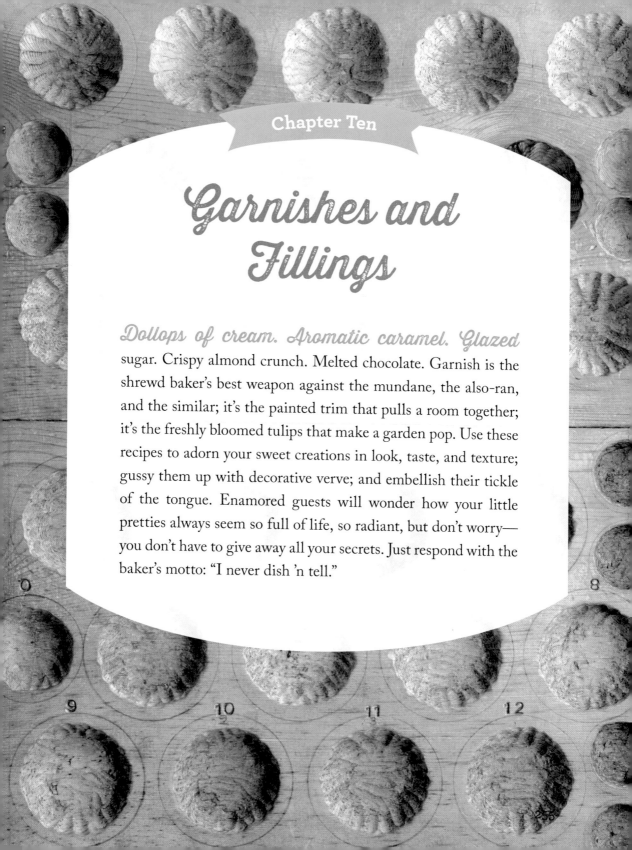

Chapter Ten

Garnishes and Fillings

Dollops of cream. Aromatic caramel. Glazed sugar. Crispy almond crunch. Melted chocolate. Garnish is the shrewd baker's best weapon against the mundane, the also-ran, and the similar; it's the painted trim that pulls a room together; it's the freshly bloomed tulips that make a garden pop. Use these recipes to adorn your sweet creations in look, taste, and texture; gussy them up with decorative verve; and embellish their tickle of the tongue. Enamored guests will wonder how your little pretties always seem so full of life, so radiant, but don't worry— you don't have to give away all your secrets. Just respond with the baker's motto: "I never dish 'n tell."

Crumb Topping

An all-around good fit for any bashful pie filling, this versatile topping covers without smothering—and truly soars with a ½ cup of chopped pecans added in.

TO PREPARE

In a bowl, combine the sugar, flour, cinnamon, and salt. Cut the butter into the flour mixture a little bit at a time until you have added all the butter and the mixture looks like small crumbles. Sprinkle the mixture lightly over your dish and bake.

This recipe is generously sufficient for one regular or one deep-dish 9-inch pie.

INGREDIENTS

1 cup sugar

1 cup all-purpose flour

$1/2$ teaspoon ground cinnamon

$1/4$ teaspoon salt

$1/2$ cup butter, softened, not melted

$1/2$ cup chopped pecans (optional)

Dutch Crumbs

Oats aren't just for horses, so take care, because this crunchy streusel topping has one heck of a cinnamon kick.

1/2 cup butter, melted

1 cup all-purpose flour

1/2 cup old-fashioned rolled oats

1/3 cup white sugar

1/3 cup firmly packed brown sugar

1/2 teaspoon ground cinnamon

1/4 teaspoon salt

TO PREPARE

In a saucepan, warm butter until it is just melted but not hot. In a large bowl, mix together the flour, oats, sugar, brown sugar, cinnamon, and salt. Add the butter, a little bit at a time, until you have a mixture that resembles small crumbles. Sprinkle the mixture lightly over your dish and bake.

This recipe is sufficient for one regular or one deep-dish 9-inch pie.

Almond Crumb Topping

They say "everything is better with almonds." Oh . . . they don't? Well, they should, so let's start a new fad right here: everything is better with almonds!

TO PREPARE

Using your hands, gently combine all ingredients in a bowl, incorporating the butter well. Sprinkle the mixture over pie filling and bake.

INGREDIENTS

1/3 cup rolled oats

1/2 cup toasted almonds, slivered or sliced

1/3 cup all-purpose flour

1/2 cup firmly packed brown sugar

1/4 teaspoon salt

6 tablespoons butter, chilled and cut into small pieces

Whipped Cream

This all-purpose juggernaut first became popular in the sixteenth century, but it wasn't until hundreds of years later that it earned its English name. I'm thinking it took that long for the baker to recover from his first taste.

INGREDIENTS

2 cups heavy cream

4 teaspoons vanilla extract

4 tablespoons confectioners' sugar (optional)

TO PREPARE

For best results, place the mixing bowl and whisk or beaters in the freezer for at least 10 minutes before using.

In a large bowl, whip cream only until stiff peaks are just about to form. Add vanilla and confectioners' sugar and beat until peaks form. Do not overbeat or the whipped cream will take on a lumpy appearance. Makes 4 cups whipped cream.

For specialty flavored whipped cream, add 2 teaspoons banana, peppermint, rum, almond, or coconut extract. For mocha-flavored cream, add 2 teaspoons brewed black coffee.

Caramel Sauce

When sugar is heated, it caramelizes, meaning its molecules break down and reform into another compound with a different flavor, which we call "caramel." So bless you, science. Bless you indeed.

Melt butter in saucepan. Add brown sugar, cream, and salt. Cook over medium-low heat, whisking gently for about 7 minutes.

Remove from the heat, add vanilla, and return to heat and cook for 2 more minutes. Remove from heat. Refrigerate if not using immediately. Makes 1 1/2 cups.

4 tablespoons butter

1 cup firmly packed brown sugar

1/2 cup heavy cream

pinch of sea salt

1 tablespoon vanilla extract

Homemade Caramels

Perfect for a small gift of appreciation, a stocking stuffer, or a personal treat after a long day. Or a short day, for that matter. You know what? Any kind of day works.

INGREDIENTS

1 cup sugar

1 cup butter

1 cup corn syrup

1 (14-ounce) can sweetened condensed milk

1 teaspoon vanilla extract

TO PREPARE

Combine sugar, butter, and corn syrup in a medium saucepan over medium heat and cook without stirring, about 8 minutes. Stir in condensed milk, and bring to a boil over medium heat. Cook, stirring constantly, until a candy thermometer registers 238° to 240°F, or until a small amount of syrup dropped into cold water forms a rigid ball. This will take about 25 minutes. Remove from heat and stir in the vanilla. Pour mixture into a well-buttered 8 x 8-inch pan. Let stand at room temperature for at least 8 hours. Remove and cut into squares. Makes about 4 dozen candies.

Sugar Glaze

A million donut shops have thrived on the back of their glazed offerings. Get this recipe right, and you'll see why.

TO PREPARE

Place confectioners' sugar, milk, and vanilla in a large bowl. Whisk ingredients together until smooth and creamy. Brush onto warm fried pies using a pastry brush.

INGREDIENTS

4 cups confectioners' sugar

1/4 cup milk

1 teaspoon vanilla extract

Conversion Tables

Oven Temperature Conversions

250°F / 120°C: very slow

300°F / 150°C: slow

325°F / 170°C: warm

350°F / 180°C: moderate

375°F / 190°C: moderately hot

400°F / 200°C: moderately hotter

425°F / 220°C: hot

450°F / 230°C: extremely hot

Volume Conversion Chart

1 1/2 teaspoons = 1/2 tablespoon

3 teaspoons = 1 tablespoon

2 tablespoons = 1/8 cup = 1 ounce

4 tablespoons = 1/4 cup = 2 ounces

8 tablespoons = 1/2 cup = 4 ounces

1 cup = 1/2 pint = 8 ounces

2 cups = 1 pint = 16 ounces

2 pints = 1 quart = 32 ounces

4 quarts = 1 gallon = 128 ounces

Metric Volume Conversions

1/8 teaspoon = .5 ml

1/4 teaspoon = 1.23 ml

1/2 teaspoon = 2.5 ml

1 teaspoon = 5 ml

1 tablespoon = 15 ml

2 tablespoons (1 ounce) = 30 ml

1/4 cup (2 ounces) = 60 ml

1/3 cup (2.67 ounces) = 75 ml

1/2 cup (4 ounces) = 120 ml

3/4 cup (6 ounces) = 180 ml

1 cup (8 ounces) = 240 ml

Metric Weight Conversions

1/2 ounce = 14 grams

1 ounce = 29 grams

1 1/2 ounces = 43 grams

2 ounces = 57 grams

4 ounces = 113 grams

8 ounces = 227 grams

16 ounces (1 pound) = 454 grams

Index

Publisher's Acknowledgements

The publisher would like to thank Crate and Barrel for use of their products in this book. Crate and Barrel items are featured on pages 133, 183, 218, 221, 222, 225, 226, 230, 233, 252, and 267.

Please visit Crate and Barrel at www.crateandbarrel.com.

The publisher would like to thank Katie Jacobs for her wonderful photography, food styling, and her invaluable contributions to this book. Please visit her website, Styling My Everyday, at www.stylingmyeveryday.com.

Author's Acknowledgements

I'd like to thank Jeff Hoagland for his help with this project, and for being my professional Rock of Gibraltar and mentor, someone who helped me soar over the ripe fields of imagination to reach a place far beyond what I thought possible.

I'd also like to express deep gratitude to my agent Tamela Hancock Murray, whose professional dedication and unwavering belief in my work were instrumental in bringing *Me, Myself, and Pie* to fruition.

Thank you to all of my friends, especially Mrs. Noah (Fannie) Yoder, Mrs. Mervin (Fannie Kay) Yoder, and Mrs. Elmer (Rosanna) Esh—matchmakers if you will—for introducing me to authentic Amish pies, and thank you to Robb McLaren and Jean Mouser for sharing several of their specialty recipe secrets with me—while the recipes aren't "Plain" per se, *Me, Myself, and Pie* would not exist without them.

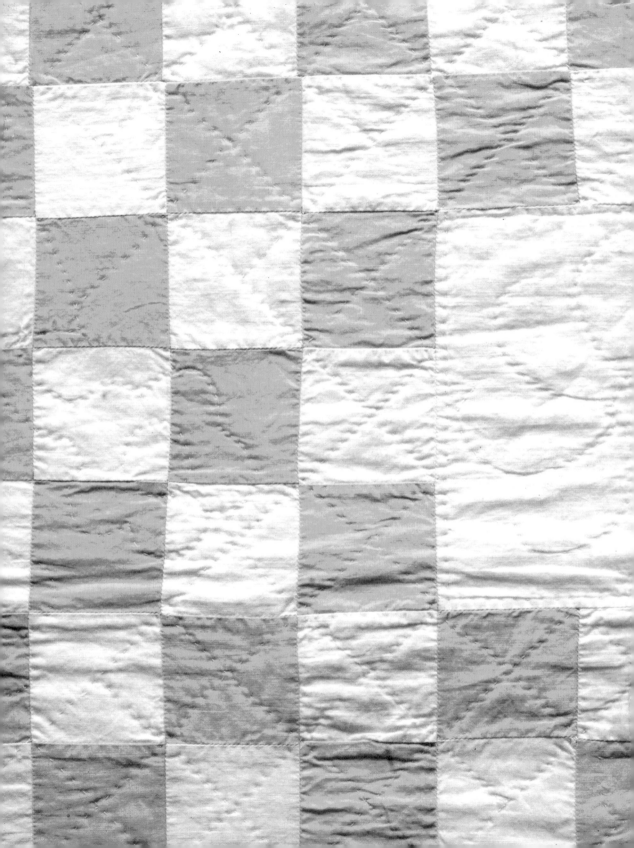